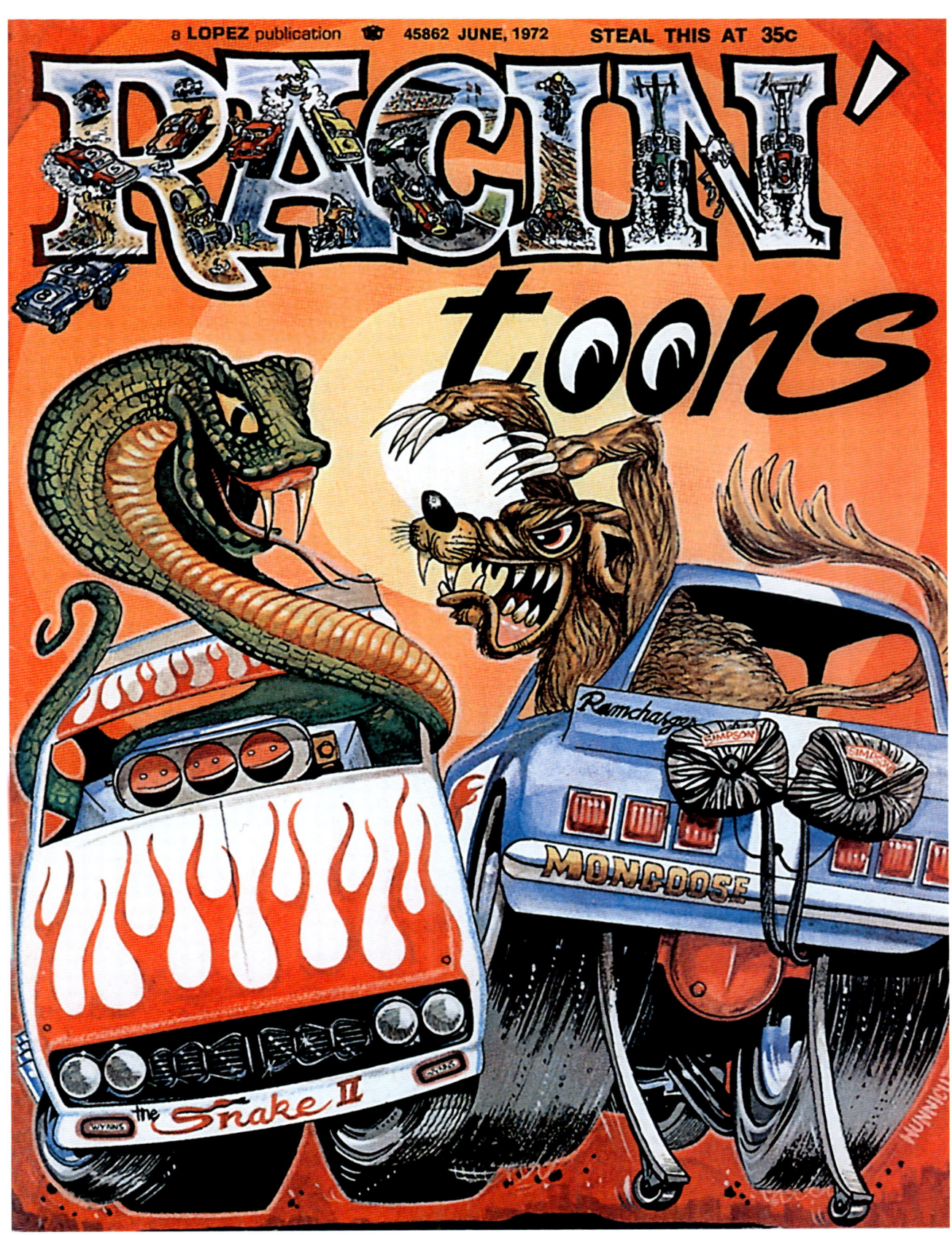

Snake vs. Mongoose

How a Rivalry Changed Drag Racing Forever

By Tom Madigan

Foreword by "the Hawaiian" Roland Leong

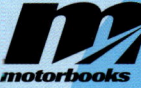

motorbooks

First published in 2009 by Motorbooks, an imprint of
MBI Publishing Company, 400 First Avenue North, Suite 300,
Minneapolis, MN 55401 USA

Motorbooks titles are also available at discounts in bulk quantity
for industrial or sales-promotional use. For details write to Special
Sales Manager at MBI Publishing Company, 400 First Avenue
North, Suite 300, Minneapolis, MN 55401 USA.

To find out more about our books, visit us online at
www.motorbooks.com.

Library of Congress Cataloging-in-Publication Data

Madigan, Tom, 1938-
  Snake vs. Mongoose : how a rivalry changed drag racing forever
/ Tom Madigan.
    p. cm.
  ISBN 978-0-7603-3486-7
 1. Prudhomme, Don, 1941- 2. McEwen, Tom, 1937- 3. Drag
racers--United States--Biography. 4. Drag racing--United States-
-History. 5. Sports sponsorship--United States. 6. Dragsters--
United States--History. 7. Hot Wheels toys--History. I. Title. II.
Title: Snake versus Mongoose.
  GV1032.P78M33 2009
  796.720922--dc22
  [B]
                                      2009014092

On the front and back cover: Whether they were running
a match race with their funny cars or a points-paying NHRA
meet with their dragsters, the rivalry between the Snake and the
Mongoose was real. So real that it led to a full-blown promotional
program for one of the largest toy companies in the world—
complete with pop art posters, cartoon-character logos, and even
a Saturday morning cartoon show.

On the frontispiece: Not only did the Snake vs. Mongoose
rivalry spawn the Hot Wheels program at Mattel Toy Company,
but it also became a cartoon series on TV and a cartoon magazine
published by Lopez Publications in 1972. *Steve Reyes Collection*

On the title pages: The Mongoose and the Snake in action,
captured in a Hot Wheels promotional poster from 1970.

About the Author
Tom Madigan has been part of the California car culture since the
end of World War II. As a journalist, he has covered all kinds of
motorsports, but his first love has always been the sport in which
he participated: Top Fuel drag racing. Madigan is the author of
several books, including Motorbooks' critically acclaimed *Fuel and
Guts: The Birth of Top Fuel Drag Racing*; *Edelbrock: Made in
the USA*; and *Hurricane: The Bob Hannah Story*. He resides in
Sonora, California, with his extremely patient wife, Darlene.

Editor: James Manning Michels
Design Manager: Kou Lor
Cover and interior design: John Sticha

Printed in China

CONTENTS

DEDICATION

TOM "THE MONGOOSE" MCEWEN:

I would like to dedicate this book to my family, my late son Jamie, and to all those children and parents who have had to deal with the deadly demon called leukemia. Also, I want to remember the many kids who carried around those tiny cars. Without the children, the Snake and Mongoose would have faded quickly back into the jungle.

DON "THE SNAKE" PRUDHOMME:

Without the kids, we just would have been two drag racers looking for a way to make a living. This book is for them. Also to my wife Lynn and my daughter Donna—without their support, racing would have never been so much fun. To Tom McCourry and my brother, Monette. Finally, to the Mongoose for all the times I beat him and ruined his day.

ONE VERY SPECIAL NOTE

During the writing of *Snake vs. Mongoose* I received a short letter from a man who, as a youngster, was caught up in the Mattel Hot Wheels phenomenon and played with as much enthusiasm as a ten-year-old could muster. I would like to share a few lines from that note:

"As children, my brother and I competed in every aspect of our lives and we each had our heroes. The two men with whom we shared our competitive spirit were called the Snake and the Mongoose. They strapped themselves behind the wheel of metal monsters and glided them down tracks of asphalt so two little boys could watch in amazement and wonder. They always played fair and, as I watched countless times, an understanding came over me about how to be a man. I remember, after the races, in the pits, we kids would gather to stare and hope to get free decals, T-shirts, or a hat. What could be better? To this day I remember that the Snake and Mongoose brought the kids excitement and joy. They came and raced then took time to be with the fans. Even though my brother always chose the Snake and I always picked the Mongoose, we were never disappointed in the outcome."

—Tom Madigan

ACKNOWLEDGMENTS

The old saw "I could not have done this without help from the following people" was never truer than in this case.

I have known both Tom McEwen and Don Prudhomme since the early 1960s and can say, without equivocation, that they are two of the best. Both Tom and Don offered their full cooperation in this project and never once turned down a request.

Don's wonderful wife, Lynn, who has never gotten the credit she deserves, helped put together all of the facts and figures concerning the Mattel Toy Company program and the inside story of what really took place.

Of course this is a book filled with action photos, and one of the best action photographers in the world, Steve Reyes, came through with over 200 of his best shots from which to choose. Photos were also used from Tom McEwen's and Don Prudhomme's personal collections, with credit going to top lens men like the late Les Lovett, the late Eric Rickman, Bob McClurg, Harry Hibler, and Alan Earman. My old buddy Ed Justice Jr. offered up a few of his best shots, and Greg Sharp, a good friend and the curator of the Wally Parks Motorsports Museum, was always on hand throughout the project offering his advice and counsel.

I owe a special thanks to Roland Leong for his foreword. Roland is the best when it comes to helping any drag racing venture, but, in this case, the Snake and Mongoose are like part of his family.

My special thanks goes to Jim White for his work on behalf of Tom McEwen, collecting information and supplying photos from the McEwen collection. Thanks to Randy Fish, one of the best magazine editors around and expert in drag racing history. To my wife, Darlene, who had to put up with getting the full treatment from both the Snake and the Mongoose.

Then there are those who gave their time and memories in interviews: Gene Adams, Pete Ward, "Waterbed" Fred Miller, Billy "Bones" Miller, Bob Brandt, Marv Rifchin, Chris Bouman, Larry Wood, Jerry Frye, and many others who just offered a word of support. Finally, thanks to my ever-present editor Jim Michels, who always put the project first. Without his hard work this would never have turned out the way it did.

FOREWORD

BY ROLAND LEONG

Author's note: "The Hawaiian" Roland Leong made his name as a car owner and crew chief, producing some of the most fantastic nitro-burning cars ever seen in drag racing. Born in Hawaii, Roland came to the mainland as a teenager with a sizeable reputation as a hardcore enthusiast. He trained under the watchful eyes of Dode Martin and Jim Nelson, the famed Dragmaster team in Southern California. He became close friends with Keith Black and had cars built by the hottest chassis builders—guys like Kent Fuller and Don Long. Roland raced with and against both the Snake and the Mongoose. In fact, amid great controversy, with questions not settled even today, Roland once hired Prudhomme to drive his dragster with the objective of beating McEwen every time they raced.

Despite their differences on the track, the three combatants have remained close friends. Both McEwen and Prudhomme readily admit that Roland Leong was a key player in the West Coast movement toward the rise of funny car popularity in California. They go as far as to say that if it had not been for racers like the Hawaiian, who switched from dragsters to funny cars, the rivalry of Snake vs. Mongoose and the ensuing Hot Wheels craze might never had happened.

I met the Snake first, or, as I call him, "the Viper," in Hawaii back in the 1960s.

In my early days, I had a Dragmaster blown gas dragster built by Jim Nelson and Dode Martin. I ran the car locally in Hawaii with some support from my parents.

In 1964, a promoter opened a new drag strip in Hawaii, and as it happened the guy who owned the strip also raced boats, and Keith Black built his engines. As part of a promotion package, the strip owner invited the Greer, Black, and Prudhomme car over to help draw a crowd for the opening. I had my dragster there, and, during the event, I introduced myself to Prudhomme. He sort of grunted a couple of times but didn't talk much; he has never been the easiest guy to get to know.

Later, I moved to California and commissioned Kent Fuller to build a Top Fuel dragster for me, and while I was installing the engine at Black's shop, Prudhomme and I became better acquainted.

The face of Top Fuel drag racing in the mid-1960s included three of the most talented players ever: owner and crew chief Roland Leong (left), legendary engine builder Keith Black (center), and the Snake (right). When asked about doing the foreword for this book, Roland said that he would be proud to offer his comments and felt bad that the Mongoose never drove for him. **Roland Leong Collection**

Once the car was complete, I tried to drive it and crashed on the first run, causing Keith Black to advise me to become a crew chief and hire a driver. The Snake and I became a pretty good team, winning the 1965 NHRA Winternationals and the '65 U.S. Nationals.

By 1965, Fuel dragsters were the top dogs in the sport, and it was nothing to have 60 cars show up for a race. However, in order to make a living or at least break even, the big deal was running match races. Both Prudhomme and McEwen had their Snake and Mongoose thing going on, and I wanted in on the action. We started match racing, and sure enough we had a go against McEwen. It was a perfect setup: Lion's Drag Strip in Long Beach on a Saturday night; Snake vs. Mongoose plus it matched my "Hawaiian" dragster against Lou Baney and the Yeakel Plymouth car. Baney had his engines built by Ed Pink, and we had Keith Black. It was two great drivers against two great engine builders.

Prudhomme was pumped up and ready. For about a week before the race, McEwen would come by Keith Black's shop for lunch and start running his mouth about how good he was. Prudhomme didn't take joking around very well and, after a couple of times, got pissed. So, by the time we got ready to race, Prudhomme was hot. It was a two-out-of-three match, and, in the first round, McEwen caught the Snake napping and put a holeshot on him. In the second round, the Snake broke the track record, beating McEwen. Then came the final, and McEwen put another holeshot on Prudhomme and beat him.

Prudhomme jumped out of the car and ran over to the Yeakel car and started cussing out the crew. He didn't talk to either McEwen or Baney from the time of that race, through the Winternationals, and on into summer. Finally, at the **Hot Rod** magazine meet at Riverside in June, the two started talking. He just hated to lose. I never had the chance to have McEwen drive for me; I think I would have liked having him around.

In the early '60s, the FX cars had made their appearance, but we dragster guys, were not impressed. Many of those early FX cars came from stock car classes. Teams like the Ramchargers, Sox and Martin, Dick Landy, Dave Strickler, Jungle Jim Liberman, Jack Chrisman, and Dyno Don Nicholson had gone from Super Stock to FX (Factory Experimental). With the engine set back, the altered wheelbase, and running huge amounts of nitro, the FX cars became show cars and brought in a new breed of fan. But we didn't care; our cars were real race cars. And, for a time, the Fuel dragster remained king of the sport.

However, by 1967–1968, I started to notice that the funny cars had become more popular with the fans and that promoters started booking funny cars for match races, drawing big crowds. Suddenly, the funny cars were running more dates than the dragsters. Remember, appearance money, match races, and tow money were how we made our living. I decided, in order to survive, I would have to get in on the extra bookings and build a funny car.

Because of a special relationship between Keith Black and Chrysler Corporation, I had an inside track to the latest equipment. So, when the new late-model 426 Hemi came out, I was the first on the West Coast to get one. I took the new engine and installed it into a chassis built by Ron and Gene, the Logghe brothers, who at the time were the most popular funny car builders.

Back then funny cars had nothing in common with today's 300-mile-per-hour cars. My first funny car had a coil-spring suspension, an automatic transmission, a dry-sump oil system, and a water pump to keep the engine cool while we did burnouts.

I carried over the name **Hawaiian** on the funny car and began running more paid dates than I had ever run. Despite the growth of Funny Car racing, we ex-dragster racers never saw the advantage of all that ad space on the side of the car. I was never a marketing guy; most of us racers didn't have college degrees and were not very good at talking to sponsors. McEwen was the smartest of the bunch. When he came up with the Hot Wheels deal using the Snake and Mongoose characters, it shook the world of drag racing big time. He produced a sponsorship package that allowed him and Prudhomme to buy the best equipment, pay expenses, make money, and sell their image all over the United States. I hate to admit it, but McEwen and Prudhomme showed us the way to the future. They were a lot smarter than most of us who didn't see past the end of the quarter-mile.

> **"I hate to admit it, but McEwen and Prudhomme showed us the way to the future. They were a lot smarter than most of us who didn't see past the end of the quarter-mile."**

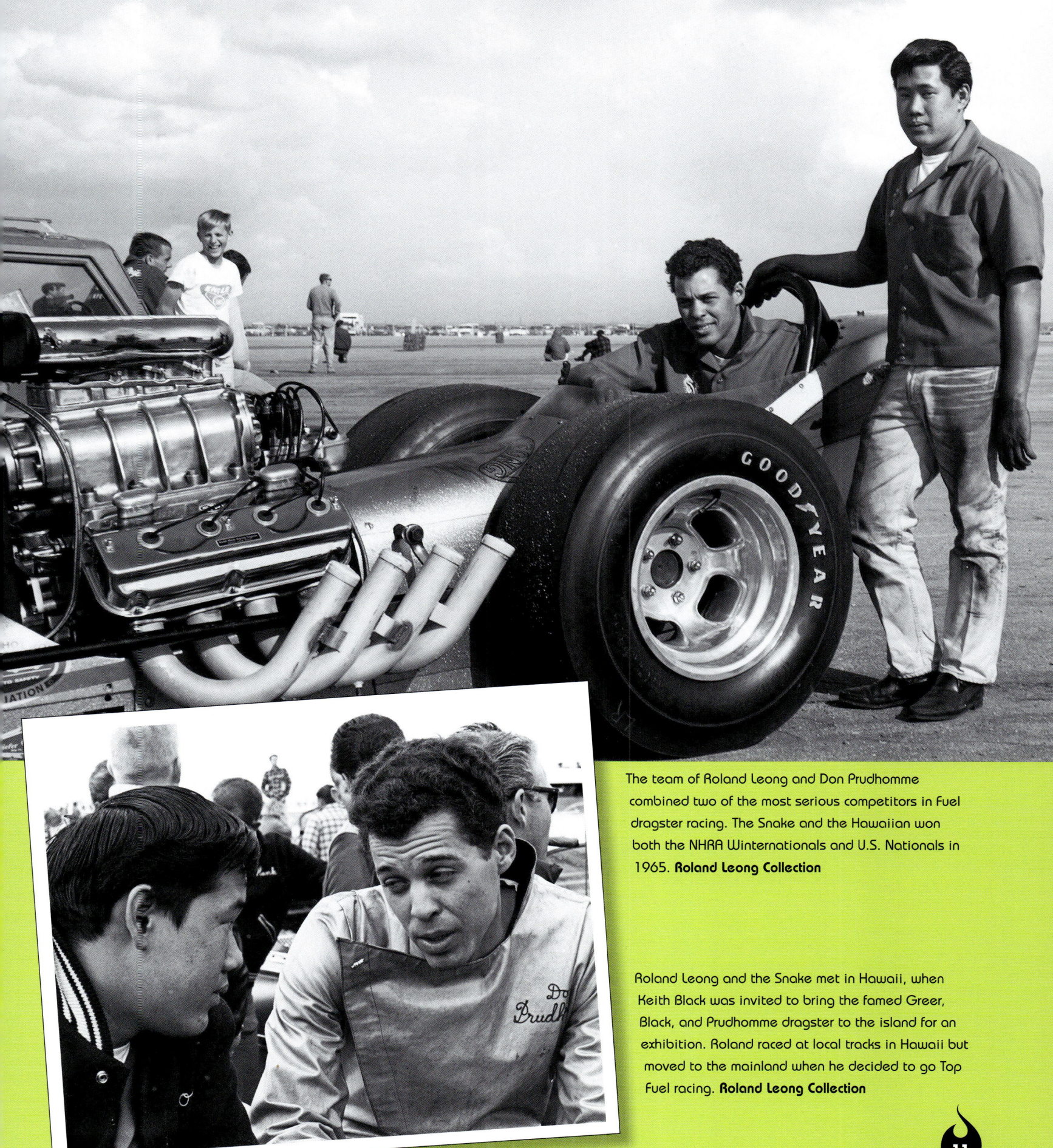

The team of Roland Leong and Don Prudhomme combined two of the most serious competitors in Fuel dragster racing. The Snake and the Hawaiian won both the NHRA Winternationals and U.S. Nationals in 1965. **Roland Leong Collection**

Roland Leong and the Snake met in Hawaii, when Keith Black was invited to bring the famed Greer, Black, and Prudhomme dragster to the island for an exhibition. Roland raced at local tracks in Hawaii but moved to the mainland when he decided to go Top Fuel racing. **Roland Leong Collection**

When the Dick Bellfatti racing team came west from New Jersey to have Kent Fuller build them a fuel dragster, **The Shadow**, Dave Zeuschel built the engine, and Bob Sorrell pounded out the aluminum body. None other than the Snake was hired to do the test-driving at San Fernando before the car was even painted. **Harry Hibler Collection**

INTRODUCTION

This book documents the accomplishments of two major players in the history of drag racing. It is a story of spirit, determination, courage, imagination, and the ability to overcome unending obstacles on the path to higher ground. Mingled within this struggle is a subplot that changed the sport of drag racing forever. Born of the simple human instinct to survive, an idea was hatched that introduced big money to a sport unaccustomed, at the time, to such a thing. In doing so, Tom "the Mongoose" McEwen and Don "the Snake" Prudhomme became the first professional drag racers to incorporate major sponsorship from outside the world of drag racing into their racing programs. Without their effort and vision, the glamour and glory seen in today's 330-mile-per-hour NHRA National Championship drag racing might not exist.

However, before launching into the heart of the story, I would like to present a prelude to the adventure about to unfold.

On any midsummer Saturday night in the 1960s at Lions Drag Strip, located in the industrial backwaters of Long Beach, California, one could witness a power that transformed souls. I wish I could offer the actual taste of the moist ocean air as it mingled with the surrounding oil refineries. Or the feeling that touched your spirit as you turned into the entry gate and chose your location in the pit area.

The pits were nothing fancy, just a mixture of gravel, dirt, asphalt, and potholes, but there was still a pecking order of sorts. The Top Fuel dragsters all congregated in their own area, one with easy access to the half-dozen garden hoses used to fill engine blocks before each run. Open trailers were state-of-the-art in transport, towed by pickup trucks or station wagons loaded with

toolboxes, extra tires, fuel cans, and ice chests. As the sun began to set, the rhythm picked up its tempo. Fuel dragsters barked defiantly as their engines ingested large amounts of nitro during the warm-up period. Eyes burned and sinuses cleared, casualties of caustic fumes that clung to the damp air.

As twilight gave way to night, the battle commenced, and suddenly the scene became surreal; drivers were stuffed into tiny cocoons surrounded by bare steel tubing that left only a glimpse of their aluminum-coated driving suits, grotesque masks and goggles, and wildly painted helmets. Smoke and fire, noise and speed, these obliterated all other elements. Everyone in the grandstands became part of the battle that raged below. So intense became the fight that even the chill of the night could not prevent beads of sweat from coating the palms of your hands.

Finally, I wish I could share the late hours after the battle fell quiet and left only the muffled voices of warriors reliving events that occurred during the heat of conflict. I wish I could share the pain of eyes raw from strain, the relief of a heart coming back down to a normal beat, and the hope that bruised ear drums would soon recover.

The battlefield has gone to seed, the warriors have grown old, and the sights, sounds, and smells have long since faded away. But, for anyone who made it there one of those midsummer Saturday nights, the memory of Lions will live on forever.

When a group of California Top Fuel or Funny Car drivers gather for a bench racing session, you will never hear them speak disparagingly about drivers from other parts of the country. An important part of the history of American drag racing was written by names like Don Garlits, Chris Karamesines, Connie Kalitta, Joe Schubeck, Pete Robinson, Gordon Collett, Vance Hunt, Lou Cangelose, and Setto Postoian, all from places other than California. However, had you asked any of these men at the peaks of their careers, all would confirm that there was something about California that beckoned them. There was a mystique about California, and an unwritten commandment: unless you raced out west, you remained unfulfilled. To the Top Fuel dragster driver, racing the bad boys of California was food for the soul. But, if you came west, you better have brought your "stones" because you were going to get tested. If it turned out you didn't have the guts, you were best off staying in the push truck.

The Fuel dragster driver of the 1960s was a very unique breed of racer. Those who came before them were considered old school, with a large percentage having roots in the dry lakes. Many of the 1950s pioneers had moved from active competition

Very few people, even those who consider themselves drag racing enthusiasts, have any idea what it was like during the frantic 1960s to climb behind the tiny butterfly-shaped steering wheel of a fuel-burning, front-engine dragster.

to the production of racing products. Other factors that played decisive roles in the evolution of the 1960s driver were the major improvements achieved in chassis design and engine development. Cars became longer, lower, faster, and lighter. By the early 1960s, speeds were approaching 200 miles per hour, and by mid-decade, 200 plus was commonplace. With this increased speed came increased hazard, and the new danger involved in driving a Top Fuel dragster created a new breed of driver.

Very few people, even those who consider themselves drag racing enthusiasts, have any idea what it was like during the frantic 1960s to climb behind the tiny butterfly-shaped steering wheel of a fuel-burning, front-engine dragster. Sitting 20 inches behind a supercharger loaded with nitromethane, all you got was blasted in the face with hot oil, nitro fumes, exhaust header flames, and the occasional valve head while you tried to control a 200-mile-per-hour rocket that wanted to go its own way. Trust me, the experience was not for the faint of heart.

A friend, 1978 NHRA National Champion Kelly Brown, once told me that when he thought about driving a Fuel dragster in the 1960s, with a driveshaft between his legs and a 6:71 blower less than two feet from his face, it brought on a cold sweat.

Teams in the 1960s raced for savings bonds, free oil, parts supplied by sponsoring manufacturers, and the chance to have their pictures in a magazine. Match racing for cash became a big deal among the Top Fuel drivers; so did clutch failures, blower explosions, parachute malfunctions, and fistfights. Drivers took on their own special images, and most had nicknames. Fans would pick their favorites. Choices included TV Tommy, the Greek, Big Daddy, the Zookeeper, the Bounty Hunter, Gentleman Joe, the Frantic Four, the Surfers, Don the Beachcomber, the Hawaiian, the Mangler, and, of course, the Snake and the Mongoose.

Anyone who ran a fuel dragster in the 1960s knows firsthand the huge influence the man in this photo had on the sport. Keith Black took performance and engine building to new levels. He set the bar as high as it would go. Black played a very important role in the lives of both Don Prudhomme and Tom McEwen. **Steve Reyes**

There's a Mongoose in the zoo! Here's one of those moments that few fans remember. Tom McEwen was asked to sub for an ailing John Mulligan in the stout Beebe and Mulligan car. **Steve Reyes**

It was never easy to make a living drag racing. Hardly anyone did, but nobody cared. Teams were made up of friends, sponsored by local gas stations or garages.

Because California is such a large geographical area, the 1960s-era racers could travel up and down the state, running a substantial list of drag strips. There was little money, so racers took on the lifestyle of a gypsy; peanut butter and jelly was a major food staple, sleeping in the back of a pickup truck and bathing in a service station restroom became standard procedure. When a few extra dollars were available, teams would rent one motel room for the entire crew; at least it was indoors. At the top of the food chain were the teams receiving appearance money or those who ran match races for cash payouts, but, still, money, or more precisely the lack of it, remained the habitual worry.

Don Garlits' wonderful wife, Pat, told the story of their early days towing an open trailer behind a used Chevy Suburban. She and Don took their children with them during the summer months—remember, this was back before disposable diapers and ready-made baby formula. Pat said she would put the dirty diapers in a container and strap them on the trailer until they could find a laundry. Garlits became one of the first dragster drivers to get appearance money. "I had to get paid or I didn't eat" was how he put it.

As the decade of the 1960s wore on, it became apparent that something had to be done about the rising cost of running a Fuel dragster. Nitro went to five dollars a gallon, new tires were used for every event, and engine parts became much more costly. "How fast do you want to go? You do? How much money do you have?" was now a reality.

Both Tom McEwen and Don Prudhomme had become very popular Top Fuel dragster drivers on the California scene. By the late 1960s, they were in demand. They drove the best machines and actually made money as full-time professional drivers. However, with the advent of the funny car and the escalating costs of racing, they knew that the days of savings bonds, free oil, and a few dollars from a rich sugar daddy were on the way out.

The two racers also realized that a colorful rivalry based on their racing nicknames was very popular with the fans, especially the younger fans. A plan was formed, and history was made.

What follows is the story of how these two racers changed the face of drag racing forever.

Here's McEwen driving the rear-engine Plymouth Dealers **Hemi Cuda** during early testing at Lions. On paper it looked great, but soon its high center of gravity and lack of aerodynamics would prove disastrous, sending it airborne in the lights at 160 miles per hour. **McEwen Collection**

CHAPTER 1

STAGING

I cannot remember what year or what month, but I do recall it was a Saturday afternoon. I was standing with Dave Sowins and Mickey Thompson. Teams were getting ready for the ensuing nighttime battle, and a few Fuel cars were in line, ready to make practice runs. It was a custom at Lions Drag Strip in Long Beach for crews and drivers to gather in the staging area when the dragsters came up to make warm-up runs, giving them a chance to check out the track conditions. On this occasion, there seemed to be a special interest in a new driver who was just starting to get noticed. The story was he had worked for and toured with Tommy Ivo, he was a member of the Road Kings car club in Burbank, and he had driven a few times at the Pond in San Fernando. I didn't know him and hadn't really heard much, so I gave the matter only passing interest.

The new driver was a tall, skinny kid with slumped shoulders and a walk like he was carrying the weight of the world on his back.

He didn't say anything to those around him, he just climbed into a very familiar car. The kid had bought the Kent Fuller–built, fuel-injected Buick dragster once owned by TV Tommy Ivo. At the time, the car carried a notable reputation: Ivo had won many races in the gasoline-fueled machine and had only given it up to build an even more remarkable twin-engine Buick dragster.

At any rate, a push truck rolled the car and the kid halfway down the strip, where they made a U-turn and headed back down to the starting line. It was a small, short-wheelbase car, and, running on gasoline, it was not very loud. The kid rolled into the staging lights and brought the rpm up, and the starter waved him off. The car hopped the front wheels slightly, smoked the tires, and moved around a little as it headed down the course. All in all it was no big deal.

I turned and headed back to the pit area, logging in my mind's notebook that I had just been introduced to a young man named Don Prudhomme. He was not yet "the Snake" or a famous dragster driver, just a kid from the San Fernando Valley who worked sanding fenders and painting cars at a local body shop. On that Saturday afternoon, those of us standing around the starting line at Lions Drag Strip had no idea the kid was going to be a superstar.

As for Tom McEwen, my introduction to him came later. At the time, summer of 1963, Tom McEwen hung out with the fast guys, the heavy hitters who knew all the answers. He was what they called "cool" back then; he carried a style that balanced between very hip and very arrogant. Where Prudhomme was introverted and withdrawn, McEwen was open and always ready with a wisecrack. McEwen was one who drew a crowd.

Our meeting came with Long Beach again as the backdrop, only this time the situation was just a little different, and far more dramatic. I was a crewmember for the team of Paul Pfaff and Dave Sowins, and their driver was a tough, rugged, and fast guy named Roger Wolford. Roger had advanced to the final round of eliminations. Back then Mickey would allow a small-displacement fuel burner (under 300 inches) like the Pfaff and Sowins car to race a big-bore gas car, and that is just what happened on this particular night. The Top Gas car Roger had to face was none other than McEwen's. I can't remember who McEwen was driving for; it could have been Gene Adams and an Oldsmobile Top Gas car. To make matters even more interesting, track manager Mickey Thompson had put up $1,000 cash out of his own pocket as an incentive. Mickey was famous for stunts like adding cash to the winner's pot, especially if it would get the track some added publicity. On this particular night, a local TV station had come to film the event for the late news.

As the two teams got ready to push off for the final, Mickey walked over to Dave Sowins and Paul Pfaff and confided that McEwen might have an engine problem, so maybe Roger should be on guard for trouble. Mickey also added that the track was getting a little slippery from the evening fog. The warning threw Wolford's timing off, and when the green light came on, McEwen left hard with all eight candles blazing. After the race, Wolford slammed his helmet into the cockpit of the car and chalked up another one for Mickey. Years later Roger told me, "The track wasn't greasy that night, but we still got greased."

Over the past five decades, I have remained friends with the "Mongoose" and the "Snake," and I've recorded various bits of their careers in stories I have written over the years. Yet, they have always been a part of a bigger picture. I went to McEwen and Prudhomme with the idea of creating a story about something related only to their careers. The answer was quick in coming.

> **The Snake and Mongoose sponsorship package with Mattel Toy Company for their Hot Wheels toys is considered by most to be the first full-fledged promotional deal in the world of drag racing.**

Although both Tom and Don have had outstanding success in professional drag racing—Prudhomme is still active as a car owner—there is one aspect of their history that separates them from all others: Based on the popularity of their alter egos, "the Snake" and "the Mongoose," Tom McEwen and Don Prudhomme conceived and executed the first major sponsorship package deal with a commercial corporation from outside the automotive industry to fund a drag racing team. The Snake and Mongoose sponsorship package with Mattel Toy Company for their Hot Wheels toys is considered by most to be the first full-fledged promotional deal in the world of drag racing. And there are those who say that without this first endeavor, corporate America would never have discovered the benefits of exposing their companies to fans of one of the most popular forms of motorsport in the world.

OPPOSITES ATTRACT

In a comparison, the differences between Tom McEwen and Don Prudhomme could not be more pronounced. They both admit freely that they have been paradoxical and even, in some cases, antagonistic toward each other throughout their friendship.

McEwen is the more open, friendly, and easygoing of the two. He is quick with a joke, always willing to help a friend in need, and will show emotion when he feels the pain of a loved one. Buried within his spirit are his fierce competitive nature, his will to win, his extreme courage and daring. You don't drive a fuel-burning dragster or a fire-breathing funny car for as long and as hard as Tom McEwen did without possessing a huge amount of bravery. But, when pushed about his abilities, he has a tendency to indulge in a mask of self-deprecation, joking that he "made a lot of drivers look good."

From day one, Prudhomme has hated losing. He hated sanding cars; he wanted to make money by driving Top Fuel

Another rare photo from the early days of drag racing at San Fernando as Don Prudhomme tries out the four-engine Kent Fuller–built exhibition dragster owned by Tommy Ivo. Ivo took a young Prudhomme on tour as his sidekick back when fans in the east had never seen a California dragster up close and personal. **Harry Hibler Collection**

Above and opposite: By 1969, just prior to McEwen taking his novel idea of creating Mongoose and Snake toy cars to Mattel Toy Company, both McEwen and Prudhomme were scratching out a living driving Top Fuel dragsters. McEwen sits on the rollers at Long Beach in his Woody Gilmore–chassis, Sid Waterman–powered AA/FD. Prudhomme waves the push truck to fire up at Fremont, California. **Steve Reyes**

For 40 years the relationship between the Snake (left) and the Mongoose (right) has been full of jokes, laughing, and attempts at one-upmanship. The two friends never quit laughing at their own human weaknesses. The contrast between the pair is what made them so popular with the fans. **Prudhomme Collection**

The Snake didn't limit his driving experiences to just drag racing. He was a very good dirt bike rider and once teamed with fellow Top Fuel driver Tony Nancy to run a Class Two buggy in the famed Baja 500. **Author's Collection**

For anyone who ran a dragster in the 1960s, this man, Lou Baney, was a mentor. Baney grew up near the dry lakes of Southern California and was a racer, a promoter, a car owner, and an all-around father figure. Baney was very close to both the Snake and the Mongoose. **Steve Reyes**

dragsters. When he rolled up to the starting line, the car next to him was the enemy. Prudhomme is competitive to the point of obsession. When it comes to racing, Don Prudhomme has nothing in his mind but victory. That drive to win served him well, since he became a champion many times over. If things didn't go according to plan, he would smolder and boil inside, angry at himself and at anyone around. Early in his career, if things went bad, you were best served staying clear of the Snake. McEwen remarked, "I beat him one night at Long Beach, and after the race he came flying into our pit area and chased off the whole crew. He hated losing."

Buried within his spirit, Prudhomme has always carried the ability to be open and caring, with a deep devotion to his family and friends. Throughout the years, he has always been willing to help those in need and has mellowed to become a larger-than-life spokesman for the sport of drag racing.

During their competitive years, the differences between the two drivers worked to their advantage. Prudhomme and McEwen actually divided the close-knit members of the Southern California drag racing fraternity.

Tough, no-nonsense, hardcore racers like Tony Nancy and chassis builder Kent Fuller accepted Prudhomme as one of their own. And the great Keith Black saw the talent possessed by the intense kid from the San Fernando Valley and gave him his biggest career boost.

On the flip side, McEwen also had his patrons, including everyone's godfather, Lou Baney, engine builder Ed Pink, the legendary Ed Donovan, and Oldsmobile wizard Gene Adams—all men who thought Tom McEwen was an extreme talent. In fact, it was Ed Donovan who convinced McEwen to become the Mongoose as an effort to combat the publicity being generated by Prudhomme as the Snake.

As for the fans cheering in the grandstands, they loved McEwen—especially the kids, who would come running to the Mongoose pit area as soon as the races were over to get an autograph. Prudhomme was more interested in racing, in winning, and in making a living than in catering to the fans. Still, because he drove so hard and never lifted off the throttle, he gained his share of enthusiasts too. When the two began match racing, and fans began to take sides, the Snake actually enjoyed those faithful who cheered for him. McEwen joked, "He started liking the fans because he didn't want me to get more cheers than he did."

When things would go bad, McEwen would joke about his shortcomings and offer up some self-deprecation to get bystanders to laugh. Prudhomme would sulk and be ready to start swinging at any sign of provocation. It was a match race made in heaven.

MARV RIFCHIN

M&H RACEMASTER TIRES

Author's note: In the early 1960s, tucked away in the small community of Watertown, Massachusetts, a father and son presided over a very successful tire company that featured truck and farm-implement tires along with the standard passenger car variety. But, there was more to the story. Harry and his son, Marv Rifchin (M&H), had a hankering for oval-track racing and began building tires for local midget car racers. From midgets they went to creating a sprint car tire, then a line of tires for the stock car crowd. So popular were the tires coming out of the M&H shop that it didn't take long for racers to beat a path to their front door.

As an example of just how good M&H tires were, take the story of how Parnelli Jones won a Midwest Sprint Car Championship in his early days. It seems that he and many of his competitors were using the popular Firestone sprint car tire, but, according to Parnelli, after about 30 laps the Firestones would start to blister, especially on asphalt or hard dirt-surface tracks. Parnelli switched to M&H tires and won the championship.

In 1967, the history of M&H tires changed dramatically, as now-93-year-old Marv Rifchin explains.

Actually, this whole drag racing thing started from the results of our midget and sprint car tire program. Some of the local boys I knew wanted me to retread tires for midget racing. I did, and then did the same for sprint cars. Finally, the NASCAR stock car racers came by, and I started making them tires. It was pretty obvious that there was a market, and my dad put up the money to buy molds, and we started mixing compounds and creating real racing tires. Business really picked up, and racing tires became a big part of our output. We even produced a logo: M&H Racemaster tires.

Then came a call from a customer of mine who told me,

"Marv you had better come down to our local drag strip and check out drag racing." I said to him, "What the hell is a drag race?" He explained drag racing to me, and I decided it was a new approach to racing that I had not seen before, and maybe I should go check things out. However, I didn't want to go and just watch two cars go down a track, I wanted to be involved.

Because the cars took off from a standing start, I figured that traction was a key issue. So, just for fun, I made up three sets of tires with no idea of what I was getting into. Nothing much happened until a fellow named Setto Postoian blew a tire. Setto came running over to where I had parked my service truck and said, "I need a set of tires." I told him I had no idea what the tires would do. He didn't care, he wanted to race! We mounted up a set, and Setto ran 160 miles per hour, faster than he had ever gone. Moments later, Don Garlits came over and wanted a set. He then ran faster than Setto. So that was how we got started in drag racing.

The next step was to have some type of testing program. So, I approached Don Garlits, who, by the way, was really sharp, and he told me what he wanted, and we built a tire to his specifications. Our original idea was to make a tire 7 inches wide, but after some thinking on the subject, I decided on an 8-inch. Don tried them, and his speeds went up, so we went to an 8 1/2-inch with the same results. From there we went to 10-inch and finally 12-inch, and the speeds kept climbing.

Our tires started breaking every track record for both ET and top speed. Suddenly, Racemaster drag slicks were flying out of our shop. In 1959, when the Smokers ran the first U.S. Fuel and Gas Championship in Bakersfield, we had a West Coast distributor named Ernie Hashim, and he was running our tires on a modified Fuel roadster driven by Tony Waters. But it was Art Chrisman, driving the *Hustler I*, owned by Frank Cannon, who won the event. Oh, did I mention that Chrisman ran our tires?

Within a couple of years, our M&H tires were on most of the top-running Fuel dragsters, but money was still tight, and I wanted to find someone who could get us exposure in magazines and newspapers, like *Drag News*, without spending a fortune on advertising space. I hired Tom McEwen, who was, in my mind, a very good professional salesman who could promote products. Everyone seemed to like him. I forget how much we paid him, but Tom agreed to promote the product to other racers and to do some testing. As things worked out, Tom, in turn, introduced M&H tires to Don Prudhomme.

Over the years, I have had a great relationship with both Tom and Don and to this day look back with great joy at the times we had. McEwen was ever the promoter, trying to pry a few bucks out of manufacturers, while Don was a fanatic about winning. I really believe that many people didn't understand how serious Prudhomme was about his racing, and they took his attitude as being rude.

Once Goodyear became serious about taking over drag racing, things got more complicated. They had a ton of money to throw around, offering teams test programs and supplying free tires. Garlits left, then came back, then left again.

The same sort of thing happened with McEwen and Prudhomme. At the time, they had their Hot Wheels deal cooking and were running a pair of funny cars. But, if I remember correctly, Don would run a Top Fuel car at the major NHRA National events along with the funny car. As a matter of fact, both he and Tommy had Top Fuel dragsters carrying the Hot Wheels banner. Anyway, one year we were at the NHRA Gatornationals in Gainsville. During eliminations, Don comes up to me and says, "Marv, I need a set of tires." I tell him, "Don, you've got a Goodyear deal, and if you put on my tires you could blow the deal." He says, "I don't care, I'm here to win, not play games." I mounted a set of tires and thought to myself, the Goodyear PR guy is going to have a fit. Don won the race, and I have a picture of Don, me, and the Goodyear PR guy. The PR guy was a good sport about it, and they didn't drop Don. That's the way he was. He wanted to win.

In the end, Goodyear outspent us. They had a test program where the teams got paid, the mechanics got paid, and, if the teams blew an engine, Goodyear would replace the parts. There was no way for M&H to compete, but I still believe that M&H had just as good or better tires.

As for the boys, they are both great personalities, and drag racing needed the Snake and the Mongoose to make the sport grow.

In the early 1960s, a long time before he joined the Mattel Hot Wheels program with Tom McEwen, Don Prudhomme (right) drove the **Hawaiian** fuel dragster for Roland Leong (far left). The pair won the 1965 NHRA Winternationals with help from M&H Tire company founder Marv Rifchin (glasses). **Prudhomme Collection/Alan Earman photo**

Once the Hot Wheels program had run its course, Tom McEwen picked up a sponsor package from Beechnut Care Free gum and built a new rear-engine dragster. From the early 1970s, Top Fuel teams began to convert to rear-engine cars. **Steve Reyes**

CHAPTER 2

THE MONGOOSE

Tom McEwen considers himself a native son of California, but in reality he is a transplanted resident. He was born in Pensacola, Florida; his father was a test pilot for the U.S. Navy during World War II, stationed near the Panama Canal. Eighteen months after the baby Mongoose's arrival, his brother Richard was born, and within weeks from having his second son, the elder McEwen was killed in a testing crash. Tom's mother took the boys to Long Beach, California, and started over. McEwen claims he was young enough when he got to Long Beach that he can consider himself a true Californian.

During the dark days of World War II, Long Beach and its harbor were Mecca for aircraft plants and military installations, including a huge naval base and shipping point for war materiel. However, outside of central Long Beach, the area remained underdeveloped, and locals enjoyed a rural lifestyle. The McEwens had some property, and Tom and Richard delighted in the freedom of open space and the uninhibited zest of just being kids. Tom developed a great interest in horses and became an accomplished rider long before he reached his teens.

After the war, California became a place of dreams. Land was plentiful, jobs were available, and many ex-GIs who had come to California for training fell in love with the place and returned after the war to settle. The automobile grew in popularity as fast as the state. Born on the vast dry lakes of the Mojave Desert, the sport of building fast cars had been synonymous with California since the 1920s, and after the war the trend exploded. Many young men who had learned mechanical skills during the war now turned those talents to

building speed equipment, and that, coupled with year-round good weather, turned racing cars into a phenomenon. The hot rod generation was introduced into everyday society.

By 1950, a new form of racing was established called drag racing. Since it was conducted on quarter-mile strips of asphalt, abandoned or sparsely used airports were considered ideal venues. The sport caught on like a wildfire, and soon drag strips were as numerous as traditional circle tracks. Anguished parents discovered their children enthralled by

the exploits of hot rodders as exposed on the pages of a magazine called *Hot Rod*.

At age 15, Tom McEwen ventured outside the box he had been accustomed to and discovered the craze that would change his life. Unknown to his mother, young Tom engaged in a clandestine caper befitting the mindset of a car-crazed fifteen-year-old. He took his mother's Oldsmobile coupe to Santa Ana drag strip and made a few passes. He got the car safely back home, and when Tom's mom returned from her out-of-town business trip, she was unaware of her car's heroic racing effort. The clandestine drag racing exploit remained undisclosed until many years later. McEwen said, "My mom went ballistic when she found out about my little secret. In fact, she and I had many disagreements over cars when I was a kid."

Once he turned sixteen and procured a real driver's license,

McEwen was on his way to building hot machines and racing, both at the drag strips and on the street. A natural leader, Tom soon had the local street racers united as a car club, named after the street on which he lived: the Marion Street Marauders.

Among the McEwen followers flirting with delinquency were future land speed record-holder, Top Fuel driver, and Wildman Gary Gabelich and Top Fuel driver and speed-equipment manufacturer Bob Brooks.

From the very beginning, McEwen stood out from the crowd. Like movie actor Steve McQueen, some guys are just cool, and in those days Tom McEwen happened to be one of those guys.

To prove the point, McEwen was the first hot rodder in Long Beach to take delivery of a 1955 Chevy two-door with the all-new V-8 engine. He installed a Paxton supercharger and took the car

After the Hot Wheels program, Tom McEwen ran a wide range of cars and sponsorship packages; among the major companies with which he was involved were English Leather, the Navy, and Wynn Oil Company. McEwen stayed with English Leather for several years, changing his funny car body from a Chrysler product to a Chevy Corvette. **Steve Reyes**

Although McEwen began drag racing using his mom's Oldsmobile, he quickly decided that he would need his own machine. He ordered one of the very first 1957 Chevy two-door sedans to appear in Long Beach. After installing an aftermarket supercharger, McEwen and a friend took the car to Oklahoma City for the NHRA Nationals. **McEwen Collection**

to Santa Ana, telling the track manager that it had come from the factory with the supercharger. When he beat the legendary Hayden Proffitt, McEwen says, "[Proffitt] wanted to beat the crap out of me for cheating. When I asked him how he knew, he said that he was cheating too, and I was faster."

McEwen began to learn the ropes, make his bones, and go from street squirrel to real racer. The '55 Chevy gave way to a '56 then a '57. In 1957, McEwen figured he had reached the point of being a "hot shoe" racer and decided to head east to Oklahoma City and the NHRA Nationals.

About the experience, Tom says, "Because I had won at Long Beach, I thought I was hot stuff. A couple of Marauders, Jim Yanders and Jim Duke, and I decided to go to the Nationals. When we got there, we found out that we weren't much. Jimmy Nix pulls in with this 1939 sedan with the engine set back and a four-speed transmission. Gene Adams was there as well as

Glenn Ward and his blown Cadillac. It didn't take long before we got beat and sent home. On the way back to California, we flipped the race car with me sleeping in the back seat. When we finally got home I realized that racing stock machines was not the answer. I had to move up."

McEwen scrapped the '57 and he and Bob Rasner bought a Fiat-bodied modified car from chassis builder Joe Itow and installed a Chrysler Hemi acquired from Art Chrisman and Frank Cannon. The Fiat was a move up, but it came with a very steep learning curve.

Tom says, "Well, after blowing up the Chrisman and Cannon Hemi, I bought a blown small-cubic-inch-Chrysler from Stokey and Reath. We bolted on a GMC supercharger and headed for Long Beach. At the time we [Bud Rasner and I] were running a two-speed La Salle transmission. On this particular night, I blew second gear on the first pass and everyone thought we were done for the night. But I wanted to do something special,

> **"Because I had won at Long Beach, I thought I was hot stuff."**

This (Gene) Adams and McEwen dragster was built by Kent Fuller and ran during the early 1960s. Shown here is a later version, since the team's earlier cars were originally Oldsmobile-powered. **Steve Reyes**

so we blew the tires up over 40 lbs. psi and soaked them in water. I went up and made a pass using high gear only. The ET wasn't very good, but the top speed was fast enough to break the track record for Altered class cars. I came back to the pits and told Rasner that I wanted to make another run. On that second run, my super trick all-aluminum flywheel exploded and lit the inside of the car like a bomb with parts and pieces flying all around me. The blast ripped up everything but my legs. It about blew the car in two pieces. I should have been dead meat. When we started to haul the wreck down the return road, [track] manager Mickey Thompson came up and told me, 'Kid, if you want to make money, kiss the girls, and run with the big boys, get a dragster.' That was the last time we ran the Fiat."

It would take a separate book to list all of the cars, partners, engine combinations, borrowed parts, and strange experiences that made up Tom McEwen's early dragster driving career. However, highlights included Art Chrisman and Frank Cannon giving him a ride in one of the Hustler cars, and a Cadillac-

powered Crossley McEwen drove in a partnership with two guys named Bader and Ferrara. Then Tom teamed with a friend named Dick Olson, bought a used Scotty Fenn K-88 chassis, installed the aforementioned small Chrysler engine, and began racing local California strips. After buying out Olson, McEwen uploaded another Chrisman and Cannon Hemi and headed east to the AHRA Nationals. Proving he could run with the big boys, McEwen finished runner-up to Ed Garlits (Big Daddy Don's brother) in the Top Gas class.

In 1960, with the NHRA fuel ban still in effect, Top Gas dragsters were getting most of the publicity. Only a few drag strips, at least in California, allowed the use of nitromethane, and these were considered outlaw tracks. Mainstream NHRA-sanctioned strips ran gasoline only. With that said, of all the dragsters running in California, one in particular was the 900-pound gorilla that everyone feared. The Albertson Oldsmobile team had its act together. With a chassis built by Ronnie Scrima, a supercharged Oldsmobile engine built by Gene Adams, and a driver named

Leonard Harris, the Albertson Olds mowed down the competition like so many bowling pins. Harris was a robot with lightning reflexes, an ex-gymnast in perfect condition with fantastic hand/eye coordination. At the 1960 NHRA Nationals held at Detroit Dragway, Harris won the A/Gas dragster title and set a new ET record in the process.

Everything came to an abrupt halt on October 22, 1960, when Leonard Harris was killed in a crash at Long Beach, testing a car for a fellow competitor. Gene Adams picked Tom McEwen to replace Harris and thus vaulted him into star status as a dragster driver.

Tom talked about his relationship with the Albertson Olds machine: "Shortly after Leonard's crash, Gene Adams offered me the driving job in the Albertson car. I guess you could say that it was my big break. So, I started driving both the Albertson car and my own dragster. Initially, I had a lot of trouble learning to drive

the car, and Adams kept beating on me for not driving as smooth as Leonard. Harris was a superb athlete, and you can ask anybody, I'm no gymnast. You had to drive that Oldsmobile by slipping the clutch and using the brake to keep the tires from smoking because it had so much power. It took me a while, but, once I got the handle, we started winning."

Drag racing being a sort of constant change, the famed Albertson Olds found its limitations as new lightweight cars came onto the scene. So, Adams contracted Kent Fuller to build a new car, complete with full body panels—including a radical rear section that resembled a shark fin, thereby leading the creation to be nicknamed the Shark car. Adams introduced the Shark at the Second Annual NHRA Winternationals at Pomona, with McEwen taking the car to the finals in Top Eliminator only to be edged out by the Dragmaster Dart.

McEwen gets out on Connie Kalitta's Ford Cammer–powered **Bounty Hunter** at Lions Dragway. **Steve Reyes**

Above and below: The idea of running a funny car came early to Tom McEwen. He drove a Factory Experimental machine called the **Hemi 'Cuda** and later bought a funny car (shown here) once owned by Candies & Hughes. The Snake, on the other hand, never really wanted to drive a funny car prior to the Hot Wheels deal. **Ed Justice Jr.**

Notice something different about this photo? Well, the Mongoose sits ready to have the lid come down on his funny car, but his brand-new helmet is not carrying his famous logo. **Steve Reyes**

After the Winternationals in February, the next big meet was the U.S. Fuel and Gas Championship at Bakersfield, California, and McEwen wanted to run. Adams hated the idea of running his gas-powered Oldsmobile on fuel, but McEwen talked him into going. In the first round of eliminations, McEwen drew Big Daddy Don Garlits. McEwen said, "I drew Garlits in round one and figured it was over. But, I beat him and the fans went wild. From that point on, although I got beat [in the] second round, in my mind I was a Fuel dragster driver. I considered myself

moving up the food chain, and I didn't want to go back to gas. We switched the Oldsmobile for a Chrysler Hemi the following year at Bakersfield, and we were runner-up to Art Malone in the final. A short time later, Gene and I decided to move on in different directions; he wanted to stay in the Top Gas ranks, and I wanted to go Fuel racing. I think my ego got the best of me, and there wasn't a hat size big enough for my head. That would change in a big hurry."

It was sometime during these early days that dragster drivers began taking on their alter egos. A crewmember for Don Prudhomme, named Joel Purcell, started calling him the Snake. Some say it was because of his quick reflexes, and others say it was because he was tall and thin. Ed Donovan jokingly proposed that since McEwen had just beaten the Snake, he should become the Mongoose—the one animal that could strike fear into the heart of any snake. Tom said, "Donovan comes up to me and says, 'Hey, man, you should pick up on becoming the Mongoose, it will make good press.' So, I asked an artist friend of mine to draw up the ugliest, meanest-looking mongoose he could think up. I wanted it ugly."

In addition to giving the Mongoose his name, Ed Donovan partnered with McEwen in a very lightweight Kent Fuller car powered by a Donovan-built Chrysler Hemi, but the team was short-lived. In the early 1960s, Lou Baney was general manager of a notable dealership in Downey, California, called Yeakel Chrysler/Plymouth. He and Vince Rossi convinced his boss, Bob Yeakel, to sponsor a Top Fuel dragster. Baney then hired Ed Pink to build the engines and employed the very talented John Garrison as crew chief. The Baney car was also one of the first to run the B&M Torkmaster automatic transmission. The Baney, Pink, McEwen combination proved to be very successful, and for the first time money became less of an obstacle for McEwen. During his relationship with Baney and Yeakel, McEwen ventured into a new class of drag racing called Factory Experimental (soon to become Funny Car) when he built a car sponsored by Yeakel called the *Hemi 'Cuda*. Somewhat ahead of its time, the handling was sensitive, and, at Long Beach, McEwen put the car on its roof—ending the experiment for the time being.

After the death of Bob Yeakel, Lou Baney transferred his efforts to another dealership called Brand Ford. Call it luck or

Above and opposite: McEwen takes the Ford factory-backed experiment, dubbed the **Super Mustang**, on a shakedown run at Pomona. The injected, Ford Cammer–powered entry ran on nitromethane but was short-lived.

fate, but at the same time, Ford Motor Company had introduced a super-sized single-overhead-camshaft (SOHC) performance engine, dubbed "the Cammer."

Ford decided to inject a few of these new engines into drag racing. A number of racers took delivery including Mickey Thompson, Jack Chrisman, Gas Ronda, Connie Kalitta, Don Nicholson, and Lou Baney. Again, Baney hired Ed Pink to do the engine building. Tom McEwen was officially listed as the driver. It was during this moment in history that the Snake vs. Mongoose rivalry got serious. Although it turned out that the new engine had some teething problems, originally the driver was suspected.

Neither Ed Pink nor Lou Baney would ever admit to making the decision, but McEwen was fired and replaced by Don Prudhomme. Carroll Shelby somehow got involved, the car was renamed the *Super Snake*, and Prudhomme proceeded to win the NHRA Springnationals. Now, Snake vs. Mongoose was for real, and, according to McEwen, his whole effort became concentrated on beating his rival.

McEwen teamed up with Top Fuel car owner Don "the Beachcomber" Johnson. Then he drove for the team of Bivens and Fisher, and the team of Dan Broussard, Joe Purcell, and "Stump" Davis. Finally, in the late 1960s, after a stint with

McEwen (left) in Lou Baney's **Brand Ford Special** alongside the Rapp-Rossi and Maldonado car with Gary Gabelich at the wheel. Between the cars (with his back to the camera) is Lou Baney, who's walking over to talk with former partner, Vince Rossi (facing camera, shown opening car door).

Before he developed the Hot Wheels program, Tom McEwen had earned his reputation as a quality Top Fuel driver. He drove for the likes of Ed Donovan, Lou Baney, Ed Pink, and (shown here) Don "the Beachcomber" Johnson. **Steve Reyes**

Rapp and Rossi and a car vacated by Gary Gabelich, McEwen had chassis builder Woody Gilmore create a lightweight masterpiece and went tracking the Snake on his own terms. Tom says, "I would track him like a bounty hunter, trying to put him on the trailer. Some track owners caught on and started putting up a few bucks for match races between us."

Of the two rivals, McEwen had always been the promoter, the deal maker, and the public relations maven. He realized that costs were escalating, and it was no longer possible for a Top Fuel dragster to be competitive without using up large sums of money. In 1968, McEwen convinced a company manufacturing pharmaceutical products to sponsor a Fuel dragster. The company chose to promote an energy product called "Tirend Activity Booster." Here was a company outside of the automotive performance industry paying for exposure on a Top Fuel dragster.

Other forces were at work on drag racing too, as the decade of "drugs, sex, and rock 'n' roll" came to an end. Costs were way up, funny cars were coming on strong, and the Fuel dragster was losing its hold on the top rung of the drag racing ladder.

In 1969, Tom McEwen bought an ex–Candies & Hughes funny car and started to experiment in the new class. He also came up with a brilliant idea. Looking at the Snake vs. Mongoose rivalry—which had become somewhat of a phenomenon with the general public, especially the kids—McEwen approached the Mattel Toy Company about an idea he thought might work. Debate will forever rage as to its ultimate effect on drag racing in particular and motorsport in general.

GENE ADAMS

THE KING OF OLDSMOBILE POWER GAVE THE MONGOOSE A JUMPSTART TO STARDOM

Author's note: Gene Adams is a legendary figure in California drag racing. Adams is not only known for his genius in building Oldsmobile engines, but he was the crew chief behind one of the most famous of all Top Gas dragsters ever to roll down a drag strip. The Albertson Oldsmobile A/GD dragster, with Leonard Harris driving, was the shooting star of the early 1960s. Although the combination ran less than a year, the car won everything in its path, including the 1960 NHRA Nationals at the Detroit Dragway. The Albertson Olds seemed unbeatable—until the tragic loss of its driver.

To fill the void left in the driver's seat, Gene Adams partnered with Tom McEwen. That pairing says volumes about the character and skill of the Mongoose.

Originally Tom McEwen and I were competitors at Long Beach. We both ran dragsters in the Gas category, and we raced each other just about every Saturday night. Then, when Leonard Harris was killed, our Albertson team was torn apart, and it looked as if it was all over. Tom came up and talked about helping out. Ronnie Scrima owned the car, and I owned the engine. Albertson helped us with parts and pieces. Ronnie was so devastated by the accident that he wanted out, and Tom agreed to buy Ronnie out and become half owner and driver. Albertson Oldsmobile felt that same way—they didn't want any part of a dragster, fearing that another accident could happen.

So, the car became Adams/McEwen. It was very ironic to me that, from the time I had met Leonard Harris and he started winning everything in sight until he was killed at Long Beach testing another car, it was only six months. Leonard won 12 straight Top Eliminator races at Long Beach, then we went back to the Nationals in Detroit and won A/G dragster, and we set low ET (9.25) of the meet. We got a new 1960 Ford station wagon for the win and figured

we had the world by the ass. We came back to California and won seven or eight more races before that night at Long Beach. Leonard Harris was a phenomenal driver.

At the same time we had the ex-Albertson car, McEwen had his own Scotty Fenn K-88 chassis (same as the Albertson car) with a small-displacement Chrysler. For a time he ran both cars. However, it didn't take long to discover that our ex-Albertson car was too heavy. Technology at that time was changing so fast that a car would only be in style for a year at the most. I had John Peters, of *Freight Train* fame, build us a lighter chassis. We became very successful as a team and won a lot of races.

In the fall of 1961, I had Kent Fuller build a chassis; he was noted for creating super-lightweight cars. We had a trick body built for the car where the body panels around the driver's cockpit pointed up like a fin, so it was called the *Shark Car*.

In March of 1962, Tom wanted to go to the U.S. Fuel and Gas Championship at Bakersfield and run in the Top Fuel class. I didn't care much for fuel and was not in favor of the idea. But, Tom has a way of convincing you to agree with his ideas, so we went to Bakersfield running the

Oldsmobile engine on 33 percent nitro. Tom was a very good driver and great leaving the starting line. As a result, we beat the great Don Garlits. I think we lasted about four rounds, then somebody put us on the trailer.

At the end of 1962, we switched from the Oldsmobile to a Chrysler Hemi, running gasoline at first. Then Tom wanted to run fuel, so we did and went back to the March Meet at Bakersfield. We managed to last a few rounds,

Another thing that always amazed me about McEwen was his ability to always be hustling parts and pieces. I remember once he put together a deal with Mickey Thompson to run a Pontiac engine. I didn't like the idea, but we got all the parts—engine, blower, injectors, everything— for free, so we ran it for about four months. In fact, Mickey wanted us to run two cars at the same time—one on gas and the other on fuel. I put the gas Pontiac in the *Shark Car*

But, Tom has a way of convincing you to agree with his ideas, so we went to Bakersfield running the Oldsmobile engine on 33 percent nitro. Tom was a very good driver and great leaving the starting line. As a result, we beat the great Don Garlits.

and then we got beat by Art Malone. Prudhomme won Top Fuel.

Tom and his insistence on running fuel began changing the relationship between us. I really didn't want to run fuel because I thought it was too expensive and dangerous. Tom had a lot of his own ideas, and over time we drifted in different directions.

Looking back, Tom and I had a good partnership. He was an excellent driver, and we won a lot of races. At the time, he was building a reputation and learning how to win. Tom was a fun guy, unlike me, who tries to stay out of the spotlight. Tom was also very friendly with other racers. When the teams from back east would come to California for the Winternationals, Tom would invite Garlits or the Greek, all the big names, to his shop, offer to let them have some working space.

and had Kent Fuller build a super-light chassis for the fuel engine. Later we yanked the Pontiac out of the Fuller car and put in a Chrysler. While we were running the super-light car, Tom had Woody Gilmore build a fuel car, and it was at this time we went our separate ways. Tom joined up with Davis and Broussard to go Top Fuel racing.

I watched Tom progress from the Albertson car into his Funny Car program with Mattel. I was very happy for him, although I laughed at the idea of him and Prudhomme as teammates. McEwen was a showman, and Prudhomme was all business.

After Tom and I parted company, I did go Top Fuel racing for a time, then back to Gas. I never really liked the funny cars; I was a hardcore dragster racer. But, the funny cars, especially the Snake and Mongoose team, put on a show for the spectators, and that's what sells tickets.

Like McEwen, Prudhomme switched to a rear-engine Top Fuel car in the 1970s. The Snake admits that Top Fuel dragsters are his first love and that he had to learn to love Funny Cars. **Steve Reyes**

CHAPTER 3

THE SNAKE

Don Prudhomme earned his way to the top of professional drag racing the hard way: he worked with his hands. When he was a boy, Prudhomme worked with his dad in the auto body repair business. He could prepare a car body for painting before he could get a driver's license. The Snake loves to remind people that he was not born with a silver spoon in his mouth, or, as he puts it, "I wasn't shot in the ass with diamonds—I had to work."

From the time he began his career as a dragster driver, Don Prudhomme has always been considered a hardcore racer. In fact, most who have known him from the early 1960s will tell you that he was known to be intense, quick-tempered, competitive to the point of obsession, and, at times, arrogant. When it came to racing, everyone was his enemy; winning was all that mattered. He was famous for saying, "Second place is nothing but losing."

Although his parents came west from Louisiana, Don Prudhomme is himself a California native, born in Los Angeles and raised in the San Fernando Valley.

During his preteen years, young Donald got his first exposure to hot cars from a cousin named Harold, who street-raced a '32 roadster powered by a DeSoto Firedome Hemi V-8. Prudhomme has always said that once he saw that car, he was hooked on hot rods and cool cars.

The spark of interest in cars blazed when fanned by Don's dad, Newman, whom everyone called Tex. Tex worked in a body shop called Ray Brooks Auto Body, and when young Don reached his teen years, it was time for him to earn his own way. Labor laws were overlooked in those years, so young Don would work at the shop after school and on weekends. He got all the dirty jobs: sanding, spraying primer, cleaning the floors. In time, he learned well and began painting whole cars on his own. It was a powerful learning period, and starting so young taught him the value of preparation, attention to detail, and the meaning of hard work. These lessons would pay off in the long run.

Those of us who were lucky enough to be teenagers living in Southern California during the 1950s carry today a special feeling tucked away in the far reaches of our memories. If you were fortunate enough to have been a car enthusiast back then, these recollections carry an even greater sense of affection. Not to slight any other location, but Southern California has always held several advantages when it comes to hot rods, race cars, and high performance. Great weather all year around, a history of racing on the dry lake beds of the Mojave Desert dating back to the 1920s, and the fact that many of the pioneers of the speed-equipment industry got their start in California—all these factors came together to form an era of exuberance unequalled before or since in the automotive experience. Plus, after World War II, hot rodding, street racing, and an overall lust for a stimulating lifestyle were mixed with a very provocative ingredient called "rock 'n' roll," resulting in a cultural fusion that gave birth to a new generation.

Looking back, the explosion of teenage hormonal exuberance in the 1950s, although annoying to parents and police, in reality clung ever so slightly to a sense of naïveté. Street racing was conducted in late hours on roads seldom used by the public. Young men joined car clubs instead of street gangs, and most unavoidable conflicts were settled with a few punches. It was the unspoken goal of every teenage boy to save enough money to buy a car, add some performance parts, and head for the streets with the radio blasting to "Rock Around the Clock," "Heartbreak Hotel," or "Maybellene." In a geographical sense, Los Angeles was divided into several distinct provinces: the beach, L.A. proper, and the San Fernando Valley. Each territory had its own style, set of rules, and favorite gathering locations.

Don Prudhomme was a member of the hot rod culture during the 1950s, and his territory was the San Fernando Valley. The principal conclave for Valley hot rodders to assemble was a franchised drive-in restaurant called Bob's Big Boy. Nothing was more exciting than cruising into the parking lot of Bob's with your girlfriend riding shotgun, where you were overwhelmed by the scene of hot roadsters, coupes, and custom cars parked in the stalls, trays of food mounted on the side window and the smell of exhaust fumes and burgers and French fries thick in the air.

Don Prudhomme was consumed by the hot rod philosophy and followed its teachings with total commitment. He began hanging out with local hot car owners, graduated to a car club called the Chancellors, cruised Van Nuys Boulevard, and finally became a member of the Road Kings of Burbank, which, at the time, was the most prestigious car club in the San Fernando Valley.

Prudhomme talked about those early days as a teenage car nut: "My first taste of competition came at a place called the Rainbow Roller Rink. It was the hot spot in Van Nuys, and all the hot cars would park in the lot and the guys and girls would go skating. The hot ticket was to have your skates modified, you know, with big wheels in back and small wheels up front.

When **Hot Rod** magazine was at its most popular, Petersen Publishing would invite the editors and racers for an annual motorcycle ride. It was always a crash fest, barbeque, and laugh-a-thon for all. Don Prudhomme holds the number one trophy for his winning effort in the dirt. **Harry Hibler Collection/Petersen Publishing**

(Left to right) Don Prudhomme, Tommy Ivo, and Don Moody.

It was a "rake," just like the cars in those days. We would race around the rink crashing, falling on our asses, getting everybody pissed. Finally, the bouncer would toss us out but I think it was there that I learned the meaning of competition.

"Later, I met up with Tom McCourry, and he got a car so we could go cruising the Boulevard and look cool. Compared to all the other guys we were punks, but we thought we were hot. Then I got a car and joined a car club [the Chancellors]. It was a cruising club, so we would cruise around acting cool, trying to impress the chicks. You had to sit a certain way, flip up your collar, act like James Dean, always trying to be cool. For me, things weren't really happening."

From the Chancellors, Prudhomme moved to one of the most influential car clubs in Southern California. The Road Kings was a club dedicated to real racing, not just cruising around to look good. The Road Kings would play an intricate part in the life and career of Don Prudhomme.

At the time, a young man named Tommy Ivo was a prominent Road King member. Ivo was also a movie actor and star of a TV sitcom for teens called *Margie*. Being a movie star allowed Ivo time and money to engage in his other passion: drag racing. Ivo was a serious player in the car culture; he had built several hot cars, including a very hot street roadster. Because Ivo could afford the extra dollars it took to build a top-of-the-line race car, when

This photo is one for the drag racing history books. Legendary chassis builder Kent Fuller (center), the late engine builder Dave Zeuschel, and the Snake (left) pose in front of Kent's shop in the Tony Nancy complex on Woodman Avenue in Sherman Oaks, California. This tr o and car won the 1962 U.S. Fuel and Gas Championship at Bakersfield. **Harry Hibler Collection**

Don "the Snake" Prudhomme came from humble beginnings. As a teen he spent his time working in a body shop sanding cars. Then he learned the ropes by going on tour with famed racer Tommy Ivo. He finally made a name as a driver in the Greer, Black, and Prudhomme dragster and went on to become a many-time champion. He paid his dues. **Prudhomme Collection**

he decided to get serious about drag racing, he called on a young chassis builder named Kent Fuller to handle the job. The car, a very simple and clean design powered by a fuel-injected Buick "Nail Head" engine, became an instant success with fans and with drag strip owners. Ivo knew how to get good publicity, and soon the Buick was featured in all of the enthusiast magazines.

During an interview, Prudhomme talked about his early days as a member of the Road Kings. "You know how you sometimes just click with people you meet? Well that's the way it was for me in the Road Kings. I hit it off instantly with Bob Muravez, Rod Pepmuller, Skip Torgerson, Ivo, and I already was close to McCourry; they were all hot to go racing.

"I had a roadster with one of Ivo's old engines in it, and when Pepmuller built a chassis for the club, I gave them the engine out of my roadster. Back then everybody built their own stuff. So, we all worked on the car and we all took turns driving it. From that point on I was hooked."

When Ivo decided to go to a revolutionary car featuring two Buick engines side by side, he sold his single-engine car to Prudhomme. But before Prudhomme could establish himself as a regular driver, Ivo asked for the Buick in his old car to be used as one of the engines in the new twin car. As compensation for the engine loan, Ivo invited Don to go on tour with him. Ivo would become one of the very first California drag racers to go on a national tour and get paid appearance money. Only Don Garlits was getting tow money for coming out west to run against the California racers.

With the car loaded onto an open trailer, Ivo took off from Burbank with a teenaged Don Prudhomme riding shotgun. Years after this first outing together, Ivo and Prudhomme would have a falling-out that created long-standing personal bitterness between the two. But, age and time slowly eased the pain, and the two now accept the fact that they helped each other build their careers.

Said Don, "Hey, Ivo was a big part of my getting started in drag racing; he helped me a lot back then and we were good friends. When Ivo asked me to go with him on tour as his helper, I jumped at it. I had never been anywhere in my life without my parents, and it would be my chance to see America. I remember jumping into the push car with about 20 bucks in my pocket, but I wasn't worried about money. Ivo promised to toss me a few bucks from the appearance money we got at each track. They didn't have crew chiefs back then, so I was "King Go-Fer." I cleaned parts, rode the push car, wiped tires, polished the wheels, whatever it took to be a part of the program. I didn't care what I

Above: In the late 1960s, the Snake and the Hawaiian put fear in the hearts of Top Fuel teams every time they raced. Roland proved to be an outstanding crew chief and Prudhomme a fearless driver. They won the 1965 NHRA Winternationals in Pomona and the U.S. Nationals, earning them a spot on ABC's **Wide World of Sports. Roland Leong Collection. Opposite:** Despite the fact that both Tom McEwen and Don Prudhomme were carrying a sponsorship package with Mattel Toy Company for Hot Wheels on their funny cars, the boys were free to run their own dragsters at various events like Indy in 1970, when the Snake ran his own front-engine fuel digger. **Steve Reyes**

had to do, just as long as I was going to the races. On the positive side of the experience, I was learning my trade. I learned how to read a track, how to set the car up, to tune the injectors, to adjust the clutch, and to watch how Ivo drove the different tracks. I also learned how to book track appearances, how to deal with promoters, and how to get publicity. I was attending Drag Racing College. It was all great stuff."

When the summer of 1959 turned to autumn, Don Prudhomme returned to Burbank a changed young man. As

Prudhomme puts it, "After that trip, racing was serious to me. I never treated it any other way."

Prudhomme continued driving his own car, pulling the Buick engine out and replacing it with a blown fuel-burning Chrysler. Don commented, "I was out of my mind, but I dug it. That car had a 92-inch wheelbase, and with that Chrysler in it there was no control. I was all over the track, but so what, you just pulled it down through the lights and hung on. Man, all that power, it was so cool."

Just prior to the agreement between Mattel Toy Company and McEwen and Prudhomme, the Snake was running his own Top Fuel car called the **Wynn's Winder** with a $7,000 sponsorship from Wynn Oil Company. **Ed Justice Jr.**

In 1962, at the age of 20, Don Prudhomme showed the world of drag racing that he was for real. The U.S. Fuel and Gas Championship held at the Famoso Raceway in Bakersfield was the most important race for Top Fuel dragster drivers in the United States. It was an ego thing, since up to 100 fuel-burning dragsters would try to qualify for the 32-car field. Everyone ran a big load of nitro every run. Cars came from all over the country, and it became a big deal because the NHRA had banned fuel from 1957 to 1962, so every top digger would go to the March meet to prove the point that nitro was king.

For the 1962 meet, Kent Fuller had built a super-trick chassis and mounted a blown Chrysler Hemi built by 20-year-old engine builder Dave Zeuschel. Fuller figured that Prudhomme had the "balls" to handle the driving chores. Not only did Prudhomme set low ET (8.21) and top speed (185.36 miles per hour) of the meet, but he won, defeating Glen Leasher in the final. Prudhomme remembered, "We won the race, and I think we got some cash, but it didn't really matter. Winning Bakersfield was the big deal, and I got my picture in *Drag News*. How cool is that?"

Prudhomme continued weekend racing, but without much of an income, he was soon back painting cars. However, in the tight-knit world of Fuel dragster drivers, the kid from the San Fernando Valley was making a name. In the late 1950s and through the 1960s, every Fuel driver had to earn respect from the other competitors. You were graded by a jury of hard-nosed, super-brave, ruthless racers who never wanted to admit that they could be beaten. In drag racing there are no second laps, no pit stops, no excuses—you win or lose in a heartbeat. You either stand on the gas or go home. When you roll to the lights, there is no slack to be cut, and if you whimper about losing, the others will never respect you. Prudhomme said, "I was serious from day one, and I never, ever wanted to get beat. I hated everyone I raced, and, if I lost, I was ready to fight."

As for the rivalry between the Snake and the Mongoose, it was still a few years away.

Prudhomme said, "I had to work, and McEwen was racing more than I was, and he had money in his pocket. He would come by the shop and want to go to lunch for an hour or two. I would tell him I had to get a job done. He would give me one of his smirks and take off, leaving the door to the spray booth open. I think he did it just to piss me off."

Appearing on the cover of the November 1962 issue of *Hot Rod* magazine and again inside the same issue is the car that changed the life of Don Prudhomme: the stunningly beautiful Greer, Black, and Prudhomme machine.

Thousands and thousands of words have been written about this car. Every true drag racing fan has heard the story of how a "bucks up" car owner named Tommy Greer bought a Kent Fuller–designed car from a Fuel driver named Rod Stuckey after the car had been involved in an engine explosion and fire. Greer had the car totally rebuilt by Fuller and Wayne Ewing, then hired Keith Black to build and tune the engine. It was Fuller's idea to have Prudhomme take up the driving chores. With Black tuning the car and coaching his driver, the car became nearly unbeatable. Soon, Don Prudhomme became one of the elite drivers in America and was now in the same top lists that named Garlits, Kalitta, Robinson, Chris Karamesines, Jimmy Nix, Vance Hunt, Mike Sorokin, Dave Beebe, John Mulligan, Mike Snively—and Prudhomme's early patron, Tommy Ivo.

It was during this same time period that Prudhomme became the Snake.

As the Snake, Prudhomme took on a new image: he became the driver to beat. His early mentor, Tommy Ivo, became a rival, as did all of the other drivers trying to make names for themselves. Among the most acrimonious relationships was the one that developed with the Mongoose. McEwen loved beating Prudhomme for two reasons: because he was competitive and the Snake was the best of the bunch, and because his sense of humor helped him enjoy the way Prudhomme reacted to getting beaten.

> **Appearing on the cover of the November 1962 issue of *Hot Rod* magazine and again inside the same issue is the car that changed the life of Don Prudhomme: the stunningly beautiful Greer, Black, and Prudhomme machine.**

When the deal with Mattel Toy Company took effect in 1970, the Funny Car entries driven by the Snake and the Mongoose were not much better than Factory Experimental cars; they ran coil-spring suspension systems, automatic transmissions, and water pumps. Later the cars became more sophisticated. **Steve Reyes**

Here is the reason all the kids came to see the Snake vs. Mongoose—a match race to see who was best. Without question, the Mattel Hot Wheels program with Snake and Mongoose was the most popular rivalry in drag racing history. **Ed Justice Jr.**

Prudhomme admits that he developed a swollen ego and that some of the drivers considered him an arrogant asshole. However, they still had to race him, and beating the Snake proved to be tough.

During an interview, Prudhomme reflected back to his early encounters with Keith Black. "I really didn't hang out with guys like Keith Black. I knew he was a trick engine builder, but I didn't put two and two together. Keith wasn't like me or some of the other racers; he had class, he wore a white shirt and white pants like the Indy car crew chiefs, and Black actually had a real shop and employees. He was kind of a father figure to guys like me.

"He called me at Kent Fuller's shop. Actually, Fuller is the one Black talked to originally, and Kent suggested that Keith talk to

me about driving his car. At the time I had nothing much going on. I ended up going down to the shop, and we made a deal for me to drive the car and Keith would take care of the engine and tuning. It was a great partnership. Keith was so good with the fuel system and tune-up that the car didn't need all the big cubic inches the others were using. And, when Keith and Paul Schiefer came up with the sliding clutch deal, the car didn't smoke the tires as much, and it made tracks down the asphalt. It got to the point where guys would call the shop to find out where we planned to race and they would go to another track. It was bitchin' because I had 'em scared."

The Greer, Black, and Prudhomme partnership lasted about two years, then Tommy Greer wanted to move on, and Black

The Mattel Hot Wheels program helped both McEwen and Prudhomme gain national recognition, and after the deal was over, the two continued their careers. Prudhomme became one of the most successful drivers in Funny Car history. **Steve Reyes**

Despite their long-enduring friendship, McEwen and Prudhomme always tried to one-up each other when making deals for sponsorship. After Mattel, McEwen picked up the Navy as a sponsor. Prudhomme countered with the Army. According to McEwen, the Army was a better deal.
Steve Reyes

Once Prudhomme got comfortable in the Funny Car class, it was "game over" for the competition. At major NHRA events, the Snake and the Mongoose had to run against the full field of competitors in order to win. Most of the time they did not race each other in the finals as they did during a match-race competition. **Steve Reyes**

was trying to build his business and could not afford the time. But before it ended, Black took the car to Hawaii to run a paid appearance race and to see some of his customers, members of the Leong family, who were involved in local drag racing. Their son Roland was running a car and making a name for himself as a driver. According to Prudhomme, he and Roland hit it off and became friends. When Roland came to the mainland, he had Kent Fuller build a car. Leong attempted to drive it but crashed hard at Long Beach. Keith Black suggested that Roland become an owner/crew chief and have Prudhomme do the driving. It was magic, and the Hawaiian and the Snake became a winning combination. In 1965, the team won the NHRA Winternationals.

The old saying "nothing lasts forever" held true for the Leong and Prudhomme team. Roland moved from a Kent Fuller chassis to a Don Long chassis with Mike Snively driving, and Prudhomme moved on to making a living on his own driving Top Fuel dragsters.

With his wife, Lynn, as his bookkeeper and business partner, Don became a partner/driver. He was offered the driving job in a Woody Gilmore–built chassis/ Bob Sorrell–bodied car owned by a gentleman named Bob Spar, owner of B&M Transmissions. Spar had developed an automatic-style transmission for Fuel dragsters called the "Torkmaster." The deal was that the car belonged to B&M, who helped with sponsorship, but it carried Don Prudhomme's name. He booked his own deals with the track owners, paid the expenses, and took home the profits. Prudhomme ran the car for a year, then returned the car to Spar, but by then he and Lynn were officially in business as professional drag racers.

The time was the late 1960s, and the story of Snake vs. Mongoose was about to get ugly. After the Torkmaster car, Prudhomme did not have any firm commitments. McEwen was driving both his dragster and his own version of an early funny car, called the *Hemi 'Cuda*, joining the likes of Dick Landy, Jack Chrisman, Don Nicholson, and Charlie Allen. Plus, McEwen was driving for Lou Baney, who had scored big with Ford Motor Company and gotten one of the new Ford SOHC Cammer engines. Baney hired super-engine builder Ed Pink to put the engine in a Fuel dragster. At the time, Ed Pink was in the process

of becoming a huge name in drag racing, threatening to unseat the legendary Keith Black. Baney, who had started at the dry lakes, was a tremendous force in drag racing. He was a car owner, engine expert, promoter, father figure (like Black), and one of the truly great practical jokers.

For reasons never disclosed, the Mongoose was fired and the Snake was hired to drive the car. The decision cut McEwen deeply, and he admits that for a long time he held a grudge. However, racing is racing, and when the world gives you lemons you make lemonade. In late 1968, Prudhomme left Baney and went back into business on his own. He bought the Don Long car owned by Roland Leong (who went into Funny Car racing), talked Wynn Oil Company into stepping up for $7,000 in sponsor money, and negotiated a verbal agreement with Keith Black to supply engines and allow the payment to be deferred until a later date.

It was during this period that the world of drag racing was about to change. The rivalry between Tom McEwen and Don Prudhomme had evolved into a crowd-pleasing spectacle, especially with kids. For track owners it was a dream come true—match racing was a big deal in the late 1960s, and nothing brought fans to the track faster than the promise of witnessing the Mongoose beat the Snake. For McEwen, it was his chance to promote deals to make money. Between the two racers, McEwen has always been the one who looked for the deal, for the promotion, and now he had a winner. It may or may not have been apparent in the beginning to McEwen and Prudhomme, but they would soon take advantage of one single undeniable fact: among all of the drag racing images going around at the time, only the Snake and the Mongoose were compatible as real enemies. In nature, the snake and mongoose were mortal predators. For the two drag racers, it was an instinctive pairing.

In real life the two humans began to take on the characteristics of their alter egos. On the track they hated each other. It was a match made in marketing heaven. Soon the press picked up on the rivalry, and kids who had never been to a racetrack were now tugging on their parents to take them.

In 1969, Tom McEwen came to Prudhomme with an idea. The story begins.

> **The time was the late 1960s, and the story of Snake vs. Mongoose was about to get ugly.**

BOB BRANDT

WORDS FROM AN EYEWITNESS

Author's note: Like many, many drag racers, Bob Brandt was a transplant from the Midwest. To Bob, California was the promised land for drag racing. His odyssey began when he met "the Hawaiian" Roland Leong at a drag strip in Ohio.

During a break in the Hot Wheels tour, Don Prudhomme decided that he wanted to run his Fuel dragster at a special meet at Orange County International Raceway (OCIR), so Bob prepared the car. After the event, Prudhomme asked if Bob would be interested in towing the dragster back east for a few more events. Bob agreed, and the story begins.

I towed the dragster back to New Jersey, met up with Prudhomme and the funny car crew. In those days, the Hot Wheels funny car was the moneymaker, and the dragster was used for NHRA National events.

I stayed with the team on tour as they worked their way from the east back to California. When we got to Arizona for a match race date, Don and his crew chief got into an altercation and parted company. When we finally got back to California, Don offered me the job to go on tour with the Hot Wheels funny car. It was a chance of a lifetime for me. What could be better—I was getting to go racing, and I began to work directly with Keith Black learning the tricks of tuning a nitro motor.

Of course, we were only half of the show. Tom McEwen and his crew were the second half. In those days, each car had a three-man crew, a custom-built flatbed Dodge truck, and all the spare parts we could carry. It was not like today, with 18-wheelers, 20-man crews, motor homes, and big budgets,

In the time that we ran the Hot Wheels program, the early 1970s, most of our races, bookings, and appearances were in the Midwest and East. During the summer, we ran Wednesday through Sunday. We stayed on the move, working long hours and hardly ever getting a night's sleep and a decent meal. When we were not at a track, you could find us in the parking lot of some motel working on the cars. The only relief came when we could camp out at the Ramchargers' shop in Michigan or stay with Mr. Gasket in Cleveland. Other than a few racers who would allow us the use of a shop, it was hard times and bad food.

Many times we would run a track, and, as soon as the race was over, we would throw everything into the truck and take off for the next stop. On many occasions we had to outrun bad weather, dodge tornados, drive flooded roads, or sweat in 90-degree heat with 90-percent humidity. Some days no rooms would be available, so we had to sleep in the truck. On other occasions, we could get one room and have to take turns using the showers, hoping you were first so you could get a dry towel. It was not just us; all the touring teams faced the same lifestyle. Running the road was tough business.

As for the tracks we had to run, some were good, and others were life and death on every run. I can only speak for the Prudhomme team, but in our case, Don wanted to win every race, and he was a tough taskmaster, so there were plenty of all-nighters. Then there was the problem of local racers. When the Hot Wheels teams rolled into a track, the local promoter would pump up the local racers to come out and take a shot at the high-dollar boys. Every racer wanted a piece of the Hot Wheels team. Not only did we have to race McEwen in a match race forum, but the local heroes were standing in line to beat the Snake or the Mongoose. It was like a gunfight every night.

We only carried one spare engine, maybe a short block, and a couple of sets of heads. Anything that broke after that, any replacements we needed had to be flown in. So, on top of all our other chores, we had to go to local airports, pick up parts, and then try and find a local machine shop owner who liked racing and would allow us to do some late-night labor.

Did I mention bad tracks? We ran tracks that could only be classified as dangerous at their best. It was our policy to show up at a track, unload the car, and then check out the track for condition of the surface, guardrails, shut-off area, and other safety issues. Sometimes the shut-off area would run into dirt or gravel roads. We ran tracks with potholes in the shut-down section. Some tracks didn't even have return roads, so you would make a pass and then tow the car back down the track. I remember one track we ran at night where the track owner would station someone down at the shut-off area with road flares so the drivers could see the end of the track.

One night in particular, Snake makes a pass and we head down to pick him up and can't find him. It's pitch black at the end of the track, and the car is nowhere to be found. We panic! Finally we find him, out on the highway, still strapped in, cussing everyone within earshot. He had run out of brakes, went through the shut-off, and onto the highway. Today, most of the tracks we ran would not be allowed to operate.

We were blessed, never having a major crash with either car. One reason was the fact that both Tom and Don bought the best parts and pieces available, and both crews did their best to make sure everything was safe.

Not everything was without fun. McEwen was always good for a joke, and he and Snake were at each other all the time about everything. Don would be up and working early in the morning. McEwen was never a morning person, and he loved flirting with the ladies. The Snake raced hard and wanted to win every time. If McEwen beat him, Prudhomme might not talk to McEwen for a week.

Tom liked racing, but he also enjoyed the promotion part of the Hot Wheels program. He set up radio interviews, appearances at shopping centers, and local TV spots. McEwen would have to remind the Snake that the Hot Wheels program was based on promotion. My favorite was taking the cars to local auto parts stores or shopping centers. Kids would show up by the hundreds; they all had their Hot Wheels cars, and they wanted to see the real teams. Don and Tom would sign autographs, play games with the kids, and give out toys and T-shirts. This was all before today's big TV market and video games. In small-town America, the Mattel Hot Wheels show was a really big deal.

The one thing that sticks in my mind traveling with the Snake was when we would pull off the turnpike or interstate to make a pit stop. Back east they have these huge rest stops, usually combined with a Howard Johnson or some other hotel chain. They were called Service Centers. We would pull in, the cars and trucks all painted Hot Wheels. People would go crazy; the kids would drag their parents out to see the cars. Tom and Don would always take time to spend with the fans, and, in turn, the fans loved the Snake and Mongoose. I knew that they would both rather be heading down the road, but it was that interaction with the fans that made the Hot Wheels program work. For me, they were the best years of my life.

As for my personal feeling about Prudhomme, that can be summed up in one little story. One year we were at the NHRA Nationals, and Snake was in the final. However, before they could run the final, the event got rained out. The race was postponed until the next day. Prudhomme told me he had noticed something wasn't right on the car and was worried that something would go wrong on the next run. So, we tore the car down to the bare chassis and put everything back together. It took all night. About 1:00 a.m., the crew from the other car we were to run against in the final came by our trailer, after they had been out partying at a local club. They started banging on the side of the trailer, giving us a bunch of crap about how they were going to kick our ass. The next day Snake spanked them good and won the Nationals. He always wanted it worse than anyone.

I stayed with Prudhomme through his Army deal and the Pepsi Funny Car program, and I left when he went to the Skoal Bandit Pontiac. But, in my opinion, the Hot Wheels program with Snake vs. Mongoose was the most fun of all.

Always the showman, Tom McEwen ran his '57 Chevy funny car for several years on tour as both a competition machine and an exhibition car. Fans went totally wild whenever the Chevy showed up because it was, hands down, one of the coolest funny cars ever to run. **Steve Reyes**

CHAPTER 4

THE MONGOOSE VERSION

PRELUDE

By 1968, the handwriting on the wall was scrolled in bold, block letters: funny cars were here to stay, and they were taking the glamour and money away from the Top Fuel dragsters.

Steve Reyes, famed drag racing photographer, major contributor to this project, and author of the funny car chronicle *Funny Car Fever*, offered his opinion on what he saw through the camera lens. "In the late '60s, the timing was perfect for the funny cars to take over the top spot in drag racing. For one thing, it was the muscle car era, and the Detroit manufacturers were heavy into promoting high-performance cars that customers could buy off the showroom floor.

Secondly, many of the top names in the Super Stock class had taken the next step and moved to FX or Factory Experimental cars, altering the engine location and body shape, and swapping plain old pump gas for nitro. The FX cars didn't handle all that good, and running fuel allowed extremely smoky burnouts. The fans loved the action as drivers struggled to stay straight down the drag strip.

"Another point was the fact that the fans could identify with the FX cars because they had a similar-looking machine in the parking lot. They fantasized during burnouts from the likes of Jungle Jim or Jack Chrisman. Because of the body dimensions, there was space for exotic paint schemes and colorful names. The cars became living characters, action figures that fans could cheer for. There was a tingle to the back of the neck when an announcer would scream, 'Here comes the *Rambunctious Dodge*, *Blue Max*, the *Chi-Town Hustler*, and the First Lady of Funny Cars, Della Woods and her *Funny Honey*.'

"Soon, fans lost interest in the dragsters. Funny cars offered something new. The cars would roll into the staging area, the tops would flip up, and the drivers, in silver fire suits, flame-retardant boots, hoods covering their faces, wildly painted helmets, and bulky gloves, would climb into the cars, light the engines, and blast the spectators with nitro fumes and smoke. There was nothing better to the race fan. Funny cars set your soul on fire."

MAN OF HISTORY

[Author's note: Throughout his career, not only has Tom McEwen proven to be an exceptional promoter, businessman, and overall thinker, he has also shown a penchant for preserving the history of his career. For the last couple of years, McEwen has produced a regular feature in *Drag Racer* magazine called

The Mongoose plans his attack on the competition during a lull in the action at OCIR. McEwen ran this Garlits-chassis, rear-engine Top Fuel dragster for about three years before moving on. **Steve Reyes**

Tom McEwen did not just drop out of the sky and become a famous driver. He paid his dues before the Mattel Hot Wheels program and had gained a reputation as a very good driver. He took over the famed Albertson Olds after driver Leonard Harris was killed. **McEwen Collection**

"The Mongoose Journals." It contains highlights and lowlights of his racing exploits, with a special emphasis on the Hot Wheels program. The Mongoose freely admits that he is not the most reliable source for historical minutiae, so the "Journals" get an accuracy boost from good friend and one-time merchandise manager Pete Ward, who does some of the writing, and Randy Fish, editor of *Drag Racer* magazine and one of the great nit-pickers when it comes to fleshing out details. The information contained in the next two chapters is both from actual tape recordings of Tom's recollections and from excerpts of "The Mongoose Journals."]

We were all looking for help in the late 1960s to make it possible to go racing and not go broke. However, significant sponsorship for a drag racing car was paltry at best. There were dabbling efforts; a drive-in restaurant chain called A&W Root Beer had a Fuel dragster, and Jim Nicoll had a Fuel car called Top Dog and a sponsorship program with another popular eating establishment, called Der Wienerschnitzel, specializing in hot dogs. Garlits had Wynn Oil Company, but that was an automotive-related product. And the rest of the better-running fuel dragsters would get deals on parts, or in some cases free parts, from manufacturers. All the camshaft makers, header companies, piston

McEwen demonstrates his mastery of the clutch with the vaunted **Yeakel Plymouth Special**, out in front once again during eliminations at Lions.

ard rod builders, clutch suppliers, would sponsor Fuel dragsters. Carrying your company name or product on a Fuel digger helped sell parts to the street racer and amateur drag racer. But, nobody had a big deal.

I had determined early in my career that in order to race and stay out of the poor house you had to use other people's money. So, in order to make a name for myself and to run a strong car, I was in constant flux, looking for that one promotion that would help pay the bills. By 1968 or '69 I had a name, had driven some very good cars, including the Albertson Olds, the Yeakel car owned by Lou Baney, a Top Fuel car owned by Ed Donovan [the guy who had given McEwen the name Mongoose], the SOHC Ford tuned by

Ed Pink. And by 1969 I had dabbled with owning my own cars—a Fuel dragster, and, near the end of '69, a funny car once owned by Candies & Hughes. But, what was important to my career at the time was the fact that I had been able to convince several companies to cough up a few bucks to get their names on my cars. The oil additive company Bardahl gave me a stipend for the dragster to carry a decal on the cowling. Then a friend of mine got me hooked up with a big-time pharmacological company, and they were pushing two products. One was called Tirend Activity Booster, and the other was a breath freshener called Gold Spot. I got a $1,000-per-year sponsorship package and figured I had hit the jackpot.

At the same time the Snake and Mongoose rivalry had become a monster promotion. Don and I were getting a lot of publicity in car magazines and **Drag News**, the weekly drag racing paper. Everyone kept telling me "you should take advantage of that Snake vs. Mongoose thing."

I started thinking and came up with an idea to use the Snake and Mongoose characters to create a toy for kids. Mattel had hit the market with its Hot Wheels collection about three or four years earlier, and my idea began to drift in the direction of that program.

At the time, my mother worked as a secretary for a law firm, and she had married an attorney named Joe Ball. Joe was a partner in the high-buck law firm that, by pure coincidence, had Mattel Toy Company as one of its clients. Joe was a very well-known and accomplished attorney; he had been appointed to help establish and counsel the Warren Commission on the John Kennedy assassination. He was a very smart guy. I told Joe about my idea, and he quickly made it clear to me that he kept the family and his business separate. He said that because his firm represented not only Mattel but a dozen other Fortune 500 companies, he did not want to jeopardize his relationship with any of them—for me or anyone else. To Joe, helping me bordered on being unethical.

I think my mom could have done some behind-the-scenes influencing because Joe called me and said he would go as far as giving me a contact at Mattel, but no further. The contact was a vice president of marketing, a man named Art Spears. When I met with Art, he had invited Larry Wood, the creator of Hot Wheels and the high priest of Mattel toys. I came prepared with a load of ideas and crude drawings using the Snake and the Mongoose as the characters for a toy line. You have to keep in mind that the names Tom McEwen and Don Prudhomme were not household names outside of drag racing, so my whole emphasis was on the characters made famous in Kipling's **Jungle Book**.

To my surprise, the people at Mattel liked the idea very much. They saw the potential way before me, and they were ready to jump. They wanted to meet Don Prudhomme.

THE NAME GAME

The whole idea came about because of the nickname thing that was going around drag racing at the time. Prudhomme was the Snake because, according to him, he was lightning fast off the starting line. My take was that he was tall and skinny and had a nasty personality. At the time, I was driving for Ed Donovan, a tough, hard-nosed racer and manufacturer of drag racing parts who loved giving everyone a nickname. Prudhomme was driving the Greer, Black, and Prudhomme car at the time, and they were nearly unbeatable—not so much because of the Snake, but because of the pure genius of Keith Black. Prudhomme was going around with his Snake thing, but he didn't have anything painted on the car or his helmet. He would just wander the pit area, bragging about how quick he was.

As it worked out, we faced off at Pomona, and I cheated the lights and left early and nailed his unbeatable ass to the barn door. Prudhomme got so pissed off because I beat him that he wouldn't talk to me or Donovan. After the race, Donovan came up and said, "Hey, Prudhomme is the Snake, and you beat him. You should be the Mongoose, because they can kill snakes. If you were smart, you could make a big deal out of it when you go match racing."

So, I went to the library and looked up the mongoose. They are about the ugliest animal on the planet. Someone called them rats on LSD. So, I had an artist friend of mine come up with the meanest-looking mongoose ever created: long claws, fangs, teeth, just super ugly. We then transferred my new pet to my helmet. I went to Prudhomme and showed him my mongoose and told him "Let's push this thing." So he painted a cobra on his helmet and we started match racing at Long Beach, and things took off like wildfire. It didn't take long for us to realize that we had something going. Pretty soon, the media caught on, and Snake vs. Mongoose became front-page news. So, when I went to Mattel, the rivalry had developed a history outside of drag racing. I pushed it because I wanted to make money.

> "Prudhomme was the Snake because, according to him, he was lightning fast off the starting line. My take was that he was tall and skinny and had a nasty personality."

THE SNAKE SHOWS UP ...

Mattel wanted to meet Don Prudhomme. I went to Don and said, "I have this idea about putting together a deal with Mattel Toy Company using the Snake and Mongoose characters and creating a line of toys. I think that it would go over big with the kids."

He said, "Yeah, sure, I think it's great, but they don't know us from a hole in the wall and will probably change their minds and throw us out at the next meeting."

That's what set us apart. I was into promotion and trying to make some money racing and have fun at the same time. Don was into winning. He was a fanatic, working on his car and racing program 24/7.

At the second meeting, I introduced Prudhomme to the Mattel people, and things went better than I expected. The Snake was on his best behavior, so the Mattel group almost liked him off the bat.

The actual Hot Wheels program had been introduced somewhere around 1965, and this was 1969, so the Mattel designers, including the creator of Hot Wheels, Larry Wood, had experience in what kids wanted in toy cars. The artists had already come up with a paint scheme and logo design, including a wing mounted on the roof. I'll talk more about the wing idea later and why it could have ended the program in a big way. The focus at the second meeting was to let us know that the cars would be based on funny cars, not dragsters, and we had the green light to start work immediately.

For Don, the idea of running a Funny Car entry didn't strike a harmonic cord. He was a Fuel dragster driver and didn't think much of funny cars. On the other hand, I was diversified, mixing driving dragsters with experimenting in odd machines like the **Hemi 'Cuda**. I had recently driven a funny car I bought from Candies & Hughes. Mattel theorized that funny cars would be a better choice for the program, offering the slab-side bodies with more room for logos and/or other sponsorship opportunities.

Once the deal was set, Don and I, along with Don's wife, Lynn, decided that we should put together a corporation. We

![Above and opposite]

Above and opposite: A progression of McEwen funny cars, from the rear-engine Plymouth Dealers Association **Hemi 'Cuda** (above), to the car he bought from the Candies & Hughes race team (top opposite), to the first Hot Wheels Duster (bottom opposite). **Steve Reyes**

Just look at the side of the McEwen funny car, and you can get some idea of how hard he worked at getting sponsorship packages. Tom McEwen was far ahead of his time when it came to talking sponsors into paying the bills. **Steve Reyes**

Looking back on the Mattel Hot Wheels program for Snake and Mongoose, it was a turning point in the history of drag racing. Tom McEwen gets the credit for putting it all together, and on top of that he was a terrific funny car driver. **Steve Reyes**

Above and opposite: Back in the day, drag racing teams didn't have huge 18-wheelers complete with built-in shops; they had to work out in the elements. Master engine builder Ed Pink (white outfit) and McEwen crewmember Allen Gillis conduct engine repairs with the car mounted on the Hot Wheels tow vehicle. Note Lou Baney, in a Schiefer jacket, looking on, no doubt making a joke. **Ed Justice Jr.**

contacted a local lawyer and formed a corporation called Wildlife Racing Enterprises. Lynn, who is very sharp, handled a lot of the paperwork and she got advice from my mom. Neither Don nor I were very good at business, so we were lucky we had help from people who looked out for our best interests.

With Mattel as a major contract holder, it was easy to approach other sponsors. To handle our expanding empire, we hired a local marketing company called Sports Headliners

Management Group, headed by a man named Bruce Barnes. They were working with other racers like Mario Andretti, the Unser brothers, and other sports figures like O. J. Simpson. I went to them and said, "Look, I got a good deal cooking, maybe we can add a few more sponsors." It was a no-brainer. We added Chrysler/Plymouth Division (Hemi engines and Duster and Barracuda bodies), Federal Mogul, Goodyear, Coca-Cola, Pennzoil, Cragar, Champion Spark Plug, and Wynn's Friction Proofing.

All the companies could see the advantages: in addition to appearing on the race cars, their logos would be on every single toy car, and millions of them would be made. The kids would play with the cars, and Mom and Dad got exposed to the sponsors. It was the most bitchin' deal you could think of, and the companies knew they would reap the harvest. Suddenly, two local Southern California drag racers had the biggest deal in the sport. For the first time ever, a non-automotive sponsor was playing a major role in drag racing.

I don't remember the exact figures, Lynn or Don would be better at the details, but I think we got somewhere around 30 grand each from Mattel, and each of the associate sponsors paid a fee anywhere from $5,000 to $25,000 each. The whole deal, that first year, was over $100,000. Lynn Prudhomme has it all buried in some old cardboard box, and she can fill in the blanks. At the time, 1970, that was huge money. The only restriction we had as far as sponsorship went was that Mattel insisted that there would be no beer or cigarette companies involved because of the kids.

In addition to our contract with Mattel and the associate sponsors, we could also book match races and appearances at tracks and keep the money the promoters paid. Plus, I sold T-shirts at the track as a sideline. Pretty soon Prudhomme stopped whining about me always promoting and started realizing that we could make some money. Things just exploded, and soon everyone wanted to book Snake vs. Mongoose.

PETE WARD

Author's note: Having missed the glory days of the Hot Wheels program, Pete Ward was hired as a front man for the Mongoose as he moved on to other programs. Ward offers insight on the years after the "Big Deal," but, more importantly, he opens up the curtain to the personal side of Tom McEwen with some firsthand observations of the character people know as "the Mongoose."

I n the late 1970s and early '80s, I was the event editor for Jim Tice and the AHRA, running all of their major races.

In 1982, I went to work for Tom McEwen as his merchandising manager, or, as it is known in the trade, "rag manager"—someone taking care of all the souvenir sales, ranging from T-shirts and hats to toys and memorabilia. At the time, we were carrying the Coors beer sponsorship on a Corvette-bodied funny car. In 1988, Tom moved from a sponsored funny car to building his own 1957-Chevy-bodied funny car, and it became one of the most popular cars ever raced, rivaling, in my opinion, his popularity with the Hot Wheels program. The car was raced in competition on the IHRA circuit and run as an exhibition car on the NHRA circuit. In reality, the '57 Chevy got more coverage in magazines and other publications than any car that I know of in drag racing. Then in 1991–1992, Tom joined forces with baseball superstar Jack Clark and created the Mobil-1 Top Fuel car.

It is common knowledge that the Hot Wheels program opened the floodgates for non-automotive companies to get involved in racing, and, by the time I became involved in McEwen's program, corporate America had discovered drag racing as a marketplace. NHRA events proudly displayed Funny Car entries emblazoned with logos from Budweiser, Mountain Dew, the Army, Wendy's, and the Revell Toy Company, who had gotten the message from Mattel that racing, toys, and kids were a very hot combination.

Of course, in my mind, the money story does not compare with the true character of the man behind the comic strip caricature called "the Mongoose." Insight into Tom McEwen is found off the track, not within the hundreds of accounts found in racing journals exalting his exploits in a racing car.

To begin with, we all have life difficulties—painful times and situations that seemed unsolvable—but it is the manner in which we confront these challenges that makes our character. In the case of Tom McEwen, he met his most difficult misfortune head-on with the courage of a race driver and the compassion of a parent. At age 15, Tom's middle son, Jamie, contracted leukemia. Like any racer, he faced the battle with all of his strength, fighting the terrible disease every step of the way. Jamie was the kind of kid that everybody loved. He hung out with the racers and was very close to Don Prudhomme. Father and son, friends and competitors fought for Jamie until the bitter end when he could no longer fight. His passing, in 1978, was a shot to the heart of the entire sport of drag racing.

There is much more to the story, and I will try and piece together the complete set of circumstances as accurately as I can. Jamie became very ill prior to the 1978 NHRA Nationals. Tom didn't want to go, but Jamie, as sick as he was, urged his dad to run. When Jamie passed away shortly before the Nationals, Tom suffered an incredible emotional upheaval—he was torn between mourning the death of his beloved son and honoring Jamie's last wish for him to race.

Somehow, and I personally will never know how, Tom pulled himself up from total despair and gave drag racing fans a lesson in pure unadulterated courage. It was the stuff movies are made from.

To complicate his effort, McEwen knew at some point he would have to face the Snake.

In 1978, Don Prudhomme and his Army-sponsored Funny Car entry were invincible and had won everything in sight. Tom was driving his black-and-silver English Leather Corvette and had been having an up-and-down season. In the semifinals, Tom got a bye run because the car he was supposed to race broke something and couldn't respond to the call. On that bye run, the McEwen crew found a little something that improved performance. Rumor had it that they had changed the rear end gear, causing the engine to run harder.

Then came the moment of truth: the Mongoose would face the Snake. To this day, that race remains an all-time classic. McEwen left hard and ran strong, beating his rival

show up, he would check to see if the town was big enough to have a hospital with a cancer center, or a section dedicated to children. If it did, Tom would visit the hospital bringing toys (he still had a strong relationship with Mattel and Hot Wheels), pictures, games, and other gifts. He would always go alone, unannounced, never allowing TV or cameras. Absolutely no press was ever allowed. To Tom, this was a very private time.

For me, the most amazing thing about Tom's visits was to witness the reaction from the kids. At first, when they would see a stranger, they wondered what this guy was going to do to them. Most adults they encountered were doctors giving them some type of test. But Tom would start joking and giving out toys, and before long they would be laughing and having a great time. Because Tom had been

At age 15, Tom's middle son, Jamie, contracted leukemia. Like any racer, he faced the battle with all of his strength, fighting the terrible disease every step of the way.

and making Jamie's last wish come true. At the end of the strip, far from any prying eyes or probing cameras, the two friends shared a private moment. That race was their way of saying farewell to the child they both loved so much.

In true racer tradition, McEwen faced the loss of his son head-on and became an active crusader for the Leukemia Society of America. But, in keeping with his very guarded personal feelings, Tom never exposed his work to the automotive press, and never tried to exploit his gestures.

As his front man, I would always get into a town where we were scheduled to make an appearance a couple of days early to make sure of the hotel rooms and track contracts and to check with local TV and radio stations about doing interviews about the upcoming race. We had Coors sponsorship, so I would make arrangements with local distributors to show the car. Then, when Tom would

through the terror of leukemia, he was also a reassuring comfort for parents. It was a wonderful experience to witness Tom and those kids.

In conclusion, looking back on the Hot Wheels deal, I remember back in the late 1960s and early '70s, drag racing was still a small-time sport on the national level. So, when Tom and Don would come into a small town with their race cars, uniforms, haulers all painted up, it was a big deal. They would unload at the local shopping center, and kids by the hundreds brought their little Hot Wheels cars tucked in their pockets wanting to see the real Snake and Mongoose. It equaled the circus coming to town. The characters became national figures.

When you think about it, the Snake and Mongoose rivalry is one of the greatest and longest-lasting in sports history. The reason was that they really faced off, they never faked a race, and both wanted to win.

Although very subtly, the cars used in the Hot Wheels program did change through the years. At first the cars were little more than FX machines running on nitro. Later, as speeds went up, both McEwen and Prudhomme improved their machines by building new chassis with longer wheelbases and going to running gear similar to that of a Top Fuel dragster. **Ed Justice Jr.**

CHAPTER 5

LEAVING THE LINE

Author's note: As the story goes, in the late 1960s and early 1970s, fuel-burning funny cars cooked more meat than the hot dog stand at Irwindale Raceway. Both the Snake and the Mongoose were very safety conscious, and neither liked the idea of getting basted by an exploding Hemi.

Most of the funny cars running back east, and some on the West Coast, were built using chassis from the Logghe brothers. Tom and Don chose a California connection to build their cars. The pair also worked closely with Bill Simpson, who was a leader in creating new and improved safety equipment. We return now to the Mongoose.

THE CARS

We went to Ronnie Scrima/Exhibition Engineering to build our first version of the Hot Wheels cars. Ronnie and I had been friends since the days of the Albertson Olds dragster. Everybody was getting a chassis from the Logghe brothers in Michigan, but I figured that Ronnie was just as smart and could do the job. The problem was nobody had the hot ticket on what it took to build a funny car. Just ask Roland Leong; the first funny cars were all a hit-and-miss situation.

Our cars had coil-over shocks in front and a sprung rear end. The chassis only had a 118-inch wheelbase. We used a modified, two-speed B&M automatic transmission. My car had a Fiberglass Trends '70 Plymouth Duster body. Don carried a Fiberglass Limited Barracuda body. I used a 426-inch Plymouth Hemi built by John Hogan of the famed Ramchargers Racing Engines. Don, who is very loyal to his friends, used a Keith Black Hemi. Both cars had the interior aluminum work done by Tom Hanna, and Cerny's Custom Paint created the design for each car.

Although the cars were, at the time, state-of-the-art, I have to laugh at the fact that my car still carried a full-round steering wheel. And, when we conducted the test-track tests of the car, we discovered that the roof-mounted wings lifted the rear wheels off the ground at top speed. The wings were the artists' idea, and they thought they looked cool, but we removed them, cool or not.

To haul our new cars, we bought two custom-built Dodge Crew Cab flatbed haulers from the Sox and Martin team. Each was specially built to haul one car, tools, tires, equipment, and crew. Nobody had anything like the Hot Wheels Haulers.

As we got ready for our first season on the road, Mattel put only one restriction on our plans: They asked that we keep them involved in the weekly racing schedule so their marketing department could set up appearances for us at large department stores, major toy stores, shopping centers, and the newest innovation to hit America, the mall.

Mattel would set up huge displays of all the Hot Wheels games and toys, then use the local newspapers and radio stations to blitz our appearance. The kids would show up by the hundreds to meet us and race their cars on the Hot Wheels/Snake and Mongoose tracks.

At first we really didn't know what to do, but the kids led the way. We would end up playing with the kids and having a great time.

It didn't take long before the Snake and Mongoose cars, games, racetrack, and other toys became a craze. Mattel actually instituted a national contest in which kids would race in local events, then move on to regional events, and finally a championship contest, where Don and I would come in and act as judges, give out trophies, and take pictures with the winners. The kids could see the real cars and meet the drivers. For small-town America, it was a big deal.

By the end of the 1970 season, we were drawing big crowds. We even had to join AFTRA and SAG, the actors and entertainers unions, so we could make commercials and TV appearances. There was even a TV cartoon show on Saturday mornings showing the adventures of the Snake and the Mongoose. Coca-Cola put out a nationwide promotion with something like 47 million coupons attached to six-packs of Coke for a discount on Snake and Mongoose Hot Wheels cars. Kids started collecting our cars, and I talked to some kid who had every toy Mattel made featuring the Snake and the Mongoose.

What all of this did for Don and me was to expose us to millions and millions of fans around the United States. We were getting more exposure than any other drag racing team, even more than the legendary Big Daddy Don Garlits, but don't tell him that.

As if running match races and appearances were not enough, we tried to run all of the major NHRA Championship events too (in 1970 there were six National events). But we always tried to run as a pair, at least for booking purposes. I remember one time, this track promoter said he could only afford to run one of us, so we said, "No thanks, can't separate the Snake and the Mongoose."

There were times when we were booked as simply a two-out-of-three match race, and other times we would be part of a special eight-car show. At National events, we had to come in and qualify with the field. At NHRA races we did not get appearance money, but the IHRA and AHRA gave us appearance money.

The most fun was at the small tracks with a booked-in eight-car show plus the local hot shoes. Everybody who had a funny car wanted to knock off the Hot Wheels team. Oh my god, local teams would do anything to beat us. But fighting off the locals and any other competitor was only part of the game; racing my partner was the other half. Both Don and I were old-school drag racers. We had come from the school of Saturday nights at Lions.

In one of my "The Mongoose Journals" columns, I reminisced about the early days when the Snake and I started driving Fuel

Little boys and girls need heroes they can look up to and admire. The Snake and Mongoose proved to children that heroes can compete and still show good sportsmanship. Don Prudhomme and Tom McEwen were those heroes during the Hot Wheels program. They were action figures who played fair and respected the game. **Steve Reyes**

dragsters and the wild times, the pit brawls, living on hot dogs and peanut butter and jelly. The drivers were crazy and the girls were wild; it was a great time. With the Mattel Hot Wheels program, we had beautiful cars, we used great equipment, and our team had uniforms. But, when the Snake and I raced, we automatically reverted back to our roots. Prudhomme wanted to win every time, and our crews felt the same. People always said they thought the races were scripted so we both would look good. I'm here to tell you that's not true. We always ran as hard as we could.

The Mongoose flashes the victory sign before firing up his Mattel Hot Wheels funny car at Tulsa, Oklahoma. Note the absence of carbon-fiber driver protection found in modern funny cars. In 1970, the driver was exposed to the threat of fire on every run. **Steve Reyes**

HITTING THE ROAD WITH THE SNAKE

[Author's note: During their two-plus years as ambassadors of fun and games, the Mongoose and the Snake toured the country from coast to coast and north to south. They faced the staggering humidity of the Midwest and South, they were chased by tornados, were pelted by rain, and spent many lonely nights driving down unknown highways. Hitting the road does not always live up to the romance outsiders associate with it.]

We ran on every type of track you can imagine: rough, short, bad lighting, no guard railings, not enough shut-off, dirt pit areas, all the things you have nightmares about. There is a DVD out called **Once upon a Wheel** produced by Coca-Cola and Mattel dealing with life on the road. It's worth the price just to see what life was like during that period. One day we would run on a track in Iowa with corn fields six feet high on either side. The next night, 300 miles down the road, a strip with lighting so bad that it was like driving into a tunnel at 200 miles per hour with your eyes closed.

We also ran the big races on good tracks, but it was still exhausting. I gave an example in one of my columns. It was after a race in Seattle. From Washington, we had to haul to an NHRA points race in Suffolk, Virginia. After qualifying on a Friday night we hauled to Capitol Raceway in Maryland for a match race on Saturday, then back to Suffolk on Sunday. Three days later we had to be in York, Pennsylvania, for the Super Stock Magazine Nationals. A few days later, it was U.S. 30 Dragway in Gary, Indiana, then to Baltimore, Maryland; Cloves Ohio; and finally U.S. 131, in Martin, Michigan. This went on all summer. Now mix in appearances at malls, shopping centers, and toy stores, throw in TV interviews and working on the cars every spare moment, and you have an idea of how things went on the road.

I can't say enough about my crew; they kept me running and prevented any major breakdowns. I was very lucky not to have any major crashes. My crew changed somewhat over the first year;

my crew chief, "Colonel" John Hogan, left and one of Mickey Thompson's crew, a fellow named Alan Gillis, took command.

The Snake wasn't as lucky as I was. He had one of the all-time funny car fires ever recorded in Seattle. It was slightly less than an atom-bomb blast, but I'll let him tell you how he survived.

At the conclusion of year one, it was obvious that we had to change our cars to a more competitive version. Funny car racing had grown into the hottest class in drag racing, and the big names were running the latest in chassis design. It was a case of update or be prepared to look bad. So, we contacted John Buttera to build two new cars. John was a terrific car builder, and both cars were extreme when it came to detail. I stayed with the Ramchargers for my engine, and Don returned to Keith Black. We also kept the Mopar bodies, only with changed colors: my Duster was now blue and the Snake's Barracuda was white.

Mattel was also picking up the pace when it came to the Hot Wheels program and developing new toys. Mattel actually became involved with NHRA and sponsored the NHRA Hot Wheels Supernationals at Ontario Speedway in California. The other great idea conceived by the powers at Mattel in late 1971 and early '72 was the introduction of a new dragster game, and they wanted us to run a Fuel dragster along with the funny cars. As luck would have it, both Don and I had dragsters that we ran on occasion, so it was simply a matter of using my Woody Gilmore chassis and Don using his Don Long chassis. The fly in the ointment was that the artists at Mattel desired the bodies of the toys to have slab sides—both Don and I recoiled and called them ugly. No matter; we had Tom Hanna do the restyle and hit the road with our funny cars on the flatbed, towing our dragsters in a trailer behind.

If I thought '70 and '71 were tough, '72 was going to be tougher. Now we had to run our match race schedule and the National event schedule. We had one thing going for us. When we ran IHRA or AHRA events we got paid to show up. We ran the NHRA National

> "There is a DVD out called *Once Upon a Wheel* produced by Coca-Cola and Mattel dealing with life on the road. It's worth the price just to see what life was like during that period."

During their tour with the Mattel Hot Wheels program, a Snake vs. Mongoose match-up did not always happen on cue. Many times the boys would have to race the entire field of funny cars to get to the finals. Shown here are some of the hot dogs they had to race: the Mongoose vs. Raymond Beadle in Mike Burkhart's Vega (left); McEwen vs. Dale Emery in Jeg Coughlin's Chevy (above).
Steve Reyes

Part of the second-year Mattel Hot Wheels program was the running of Top Fuel dragsters. The cars featured high slab rear body panels and were part of a set called **Mongoose & Snake Wild Wheelie** racers. The Snake gets ready to make a pass at Irwindale Raceway. **Steve Reyes**

events for our sponsor's promotion and for national media coverage. And, as the funny cars grew in number, our chances of racing each other in a national event became a hit-or-miss proposition at the very best. Every name car—Chi-Town, Blue Max, Jungle Jim, Kenny Bernstein, Mickey Thompson, Gene Snow, Pat Foster, Barry Setzer—they all wanted a piece of the Snake and the Mongoose. And, if we qualified for Top Fuel, we had to face Garlits, the Greek, Kalitta, and all the rest. The Snake vs. Mongoose in major races became a rare thing, but it did happen. Example: The Last Drag Race, held at Long Beach in 1972. I managed to get to the final in Funny Car and face the Snake. Nothing could have been cooler or more exciting. We both grew up at Lions, and this would be the last time anyone ran down the asphalt strip built by Mickey Thompson.

I blew the Snake's dress up and got the win, running a best time 6.39 ET and 225.02 miles per hour. Who said the Snake always wins?

Touring the country during the Hot Wheels program was tough, but I will never complain because with the sponsorship of Mattel and the other sponsors, we had the finances to buy the best parts, put on a great show, stay in clean upscale motels, eat good food, and present a top-of-the-line show for the fans.

IT WAS NOT A MARRIAGE MADE IN HEAVEN

[Author's note: Being on the road 24/7 can become a strain on relationships during the best of times. Throw in sleep deprivation, overwork, giant egos, nagging, sniping, bad jokes, constant danger, and bad tempers, and the situation takes on new meaning.]

Don and I were the most competitive when it came to racing each other. It was as bad as the real snake and mongoose in the jungle trying to kill each other. He had to win, and his ego could get bruised in so many ways. It got so bad that we almost split up a couple of times. When **Hot Rod** magazine came out with the August 1970 cover with my first Hot Wheels car and hauler carrying the cover blurb "Tom 'Mongoose' McEwen tours his Hot Wheels" and they didn't include him, he went berserk. I didn't even know they were running the cover. He said I was trying to make him look bad. I told him he was full of crap.

I was into working with our sponsors and doing PR; it was something that I enjoyed. Prudhomme did it because he had to. The only time he had his good face on was when the kids showed up. He did love the kids. But, at the track, he was so focused that he didn't even know I was his partner. It was contagious; I started to get just like him and wanted to win every race. Our crews worked their butts off so we could get after each other. Every race we ran he had to run the engine on kill. The smart way would have been

to say "let's run 30 or 40 percent nitro and save the equipment." But, no, he ran 80 percent every round. His motto was "I'll tear your heart out on every time I race you."

One of my favorite stories about the Snake and his personality took place at a PRA race. Don Garlits had broken away from the NHRA to become a major player, along with Doug Kruse, in forming the Professional Racers Association. I had come up with the name and had worked with the organization to get bigger purses for professional racers. Garlits, in turn, got our good buddy Jim Tice to put on a race in Tulsa with a huge purse for the Fuel dragsters and funny cars.

Oh, man, it was like Bakersfield in the mid-1950s, with 64 Top Fuel cars and 64 Funny Cars. The qualifying was insane; they ran cars on Thursday and Friday nights until midnight. I qualified my blue car and Snake his white car, and I ended up low qualifier for the meet. The eliminations were unreal; guys were blowing engines, and there were fires and cars bouncing off the guard railings. Finally it boiled down to the last four or five cars in Funny Car. I remember Raymond Beadle was one, and me and the Snake. I can't remember the other cars.

It was, like, midnight, the track was oiled down, everybody was tired, and the cars were beat to crap. So, we all got together and said, "Hey, there's a lot of money up, so why don't we split it equal and then race for the win, but, if you break, you'll still come out with something." Everybody agreed but Snake. He wanted to run for the whole deal. Then he went back to his car in the pits and discovered it was hurting worse than he figured, so then he wanted back in on the deal. Everyone said "Screw you!" and he got pissed. I talked everybody into agreeing and let the Snake back in. We ran the eliminations, and Snake blew an engine and I ended up winning. We split the money up, but about half of the contingency money sponsors didn't pay, and all the guys, including Snake, were on my butt wanting their money. I discovered it doesn't pay to be nice, or as some say, no good deed should go unpunished.

The slab-side front-engine dragsters didn't last long. After I witnessed Don Garlits blow his Fuel dragster in half and nearly rip his foot to shreds at Long Beach, it was clear to me that front-engine dragsters were getting too dangerous. When I went to see Big Daddy in the hospital, my feelings were confirmed. The greatest innovator in drag racing lay suffering because the sport had outgrown its own technology. Garlits would return to the sport with a new concept: never again would he stare down the barrel of a blown Fuel Hemi. Garlits introduced the rear-engine Top Fuel dragster, and the world followed.

Because the slab-sided dragsters didn't run as well as we wanted and because we now had extra funds to allow for expansion,

By 1972, McEwen had traded the slab-side front-engine dragster for a rear-engine model, still carrying the Hot Wheels logo. The unusual point about this car is that the chassis is a Don Garlits chassis, one of the few ever sold to an outsider. The car ran several years, carrying, at various times, Hot Wheels, Carefree Gum, English Leather, and Navy sponsorship packages. **Steve Reyes**

both Don and I went to rear-engine dragsters. I bought one of the few Garlits chassis he ever released. The car was awesome, and coupled with the Buttera chassis on the funny car, we had a very competitive team. If I remember correctly, Snake had Kent Fuller build a rear-engine car that was so lightweight somebody nicknamed it the **Yellow Feather**.

Then we headed for the 1972 U.S. Fuel and Gas Championship at Bakersfield. Say whatever you want about the NHRA Nationals or any other big race: when it comes to driver ego, bragging rights or who's the big dog, Bakersfield was the benchmark. Garlits had won several; the Snake never let me forget he did it in 1962. My buddy Tony Nancy took it all in 1970. And, in 1972, I joined the club, qualifying number one, setting low ET and top speed of the meet, and winning overall. I tell the Snake that he won a lot of little races, but I won the big ones.

The Hot Wheels deal officially lasted about three years, although we stayed with Mattel longer and they became an associate sponsor. In fact, we still have a great relationship with Mattel, with 2010 being the 40th anniversary of the Hot Wheels program.

Following Mattel becoming an associate sponsor, I put together a package with Beechnut Gum Company to carry their Care Free gum logo. Snake would be one flavor and I would be the other. The program lasted only a year; things didn't work out as expected, and Don and I began to drift in opposite directions. He ended up with a sponsor package with the U.S. Army, and I got the Navy. My deal was just for promotion and PR with a small amount of money. The Snake got a better deal with the Army, and he went on to become a major force in the Funny Car class.

Looking back on the Mattel Hot Wheels program, the rivalry was real, just like the animals. It was the Prudhomme personality that made the idea work. He took on the characteristics of a snake: quick-tempered, mean, and not all that easy to get close to. Fans, especially the kids, loved the idea of the Snake and the Mongoose fighting all the time. Some kids loved the Snake, and others the Mongoose; nobody was neutral. It was a great time for both of us, and it made our careers.

> "Some kids loved the Snake, and others the Mongoose; nobody was neutral. It was a great time for both of us, and it made our careers."

A SPECIAL NOTE

[Author's note: After offering his version of the Hot Wheels program, Tom McEwen grew serious, and the constant smirk always underlying his remarks disappeared. He said he had one personal story with which to conclude the Snake vs. Mongoose era. Why not?]

You know, Prudhomme and I have had our good times and our bad times. Nowadays we are a little like Felix and Oscar, the Odd Couple. Over the years, we have had our arguments, and we still never pass up an opportunity to rag on each other. The reality over the years for both of us is that life would be less fun without the Snake vs. Mongoose rivalry. But, in 1978, at the NHRA Nationals at Indy, I believe we sort of defined our friendship and came to our own understanding. At the time I was running the English Leather–sponsored Corvette funny car. My son, Jamie, who had been very ill, died of leukemia, and I was having a terrible time coping with my decision to come to the Nationals. I did it for Jamie because it was one of his last requests.

That year, Prudhomme was tough to beat; he had won a bunch of races in a row and his car was running like it was on rails. As fate presented the scenario, I got a bye run in the semifinals and faced the Snake in the final. An old and dear friend of mine named Billy "Bones" Miller was a partial sponsor of my car with his string of restaurants called Sizzler Steak Houses. Billy was also a member of the crew, and he and I tried to come up with a secret weapon to try and beat the Snake. We came up with a trick I learned running all those slick, greasy, junk tracks when we were on tour. Everyone in Funny Car was using a 4.10 rear end gear, so I changed to a 4.33, which would twist the engine to higher rpm but get the ET down and the top speed up quicker. I rolled to the starting line, and my heart was pounding, my mouth was dry, and for the first time in many years, I felt a sense of anxiety.

One instant later I was leaving hard. I ended up winning. I yanked the chute and ended up in the grass at the side of the track near the end of the shut-down area. I was crying and just couldn't hold my emotions in any longer. The next thing I knew the Snake

Above: Always the promoter, Tom McEwen moved on after the Hot Wheels program into a series of deals with major corporations. One of his most successful was a long-term relationship with Coors beer. McEwen moved from a Chrysler body to a Corvette and soon was matching his skill against other beer wagons like the **Budweiser King**. Steve Reyes

Right: Not one to sit around and wait for a break, Tom McEwen signed an agreement with English Leather, a popular men's aftershave, to sponsor his funny car after the Hot Wheels program ran its course. The Mongoose also switched from his familiar Plymouth Duster–bodied funny car to a Corvette. **Steve Reyes**

Above and left: In late 1972 and for a couple of years after, Tom McEwen ran a Don Garlits–chassis, rear–engine fuel dragster. His ability to hold onto great sponsor relationships allowed him to take many of the companies that had been involved in the Mattel Hot Wheels program along with his efforts: included were Mattel and Coca-Cola, Wynn's, and Goodyear.
Steve Reyes

Above and opposite: Drag racing is a dangerous world, but under the fame and glory of the Snake and Mongoose there is a human story that shows just how tough life can be. Tom McEwen lost his son Jamie to the terrible effects of leukemia just prior to the NHRA Nationals at Indianapolis. Despite a broken heart, the Mongoose won the race for his son. **McEwen Collection**

Above and opposite: When rear-engine dragsters hit the sport, both McEwen and Prudhomme were quick to make the change. The super-lightweight cars shown in these photos came after the Hot Wheels program had run its course and the boys were moving on with the remaining years of their driving careers. **Steve Reyes**

was sliding to a stop in the grass; he jumped out of his car and ran over to me. My crew lifted the body of my car, and Snake came under the lid and put his arm around me. It was a sad day; Don loved Jamie as much as I did, and on that day he proved to me how much our friendship meant. It was a private thing. I never told many people, and neither did he. It only meant something to the two of us.

The end-all to the Mattel Hot Wheels story is that it made both of us household names and got us known all over the country. The

rivalry was the real deal, and the fans picked up on it. I would tell magazine reporters, "He won more races because I was saving myself for the big ones." Or I would tell them, "Remember a snake is always a snake."

He would read what I said, and it would piss him off enough to keep his edge. He wanted to beat me every time. He probably wanted to beat me more than he did Garlits. It was all great sport. Now we go to lunch, he calls all the time just so I can tell him how great he was. The Snake vs. Mongoose thing will never die. Good stuff.

BILLY "BONES" MILLER

Author's note: On the subject of his nickname, Billy said, "When McEwen was driving the Yeakel Plymouth for Lou Baney, one night at Long Beach Lou started calling me 'Bones.' I have no idea to this day why he did, but the name stuck."

The very first time I met Tom McEwen was back in 1955, at the home of a racer named Junior Thompson. McEwen was working on putting a high-performance cam in his mother's 1955 Oldsmobile so he could take it to the drag races—of course he never mentioned a word of his actions to his mom.

As for Prudhomme, our meeting came about in either 1960 or '61; Keith Black had him driving the Greer, Black, and Prudhomme car.

My own personal involvement with drag racing goes way back to C. J. Hart and the old Santa Ana strip. Nobody had any money, so we just hopped up the cars we drove on the street and took them to the drags on Sunday. Like

Jim Garner, and Steve McQueen. It was great fun to bench race with that crowd because racing was always the topic and not movies.

It wasn't until the Snake and Mongoose faded out of their Hot Wheels deal that I got into sponsorship with McEwen on his funny. He had gone from Hot Wheels to Care Free gum, then the Navy and Coors; it was during this time that I worked with him on a limited basis.

My biggest deal with Tom McEwen had nothing to do with drag racing but, rather, with bicycles. A partner and friend of mine named Skip Hess had invented and developed a cast-magnesium wheel for bicycles called "Moto-Mag," and eventually we got into building motocross-style bicycles. Then the Mongoose allowed me to use

My biggest deal with Tom McEwen had nothing to do with drag racing but, rather, with bicycles.

many other hot rodders in Southern California, being crazy for cars gave way to earning a living. I drifted away from drag racing and eventually got into the restaurant business, first with a Jack-in-the-Box fast food location and then 12 Sizzler Steak House franchises. By this time, Tom and Don had changed the face of drag racing with the Hot Wheels program, and I decided that I wanted back into the sport.

The really strange thing about my return to drag racing was that I got involved with my old buddy Tony Nancy, who had just completed his first ever Top Fuel dragster. We made a deal, and he put the Sizzler logo on the car, along with Wynn's Oil and Superior Industries. Tony had a shop on Woodman Avenue in the San Fernando Valley, and it was a hangout for guys like Prudhomme, McEwen,

his logo on the bicycles, and they became "Mongoose Motocross" bikes.

Tom has always been the carefree promoter, and the Snake, when he was racing, was as mean as his namesake. In his time, Prudhomme was the best in the business. However, without Tom, their act would have never been so much fun.

McEwen started selling T-shirts and hats at the races, and Prudhomme told him, "You're not going to get anywhere doing that. You have to dedicate yourself to winning races." McEwen answered, "I'm doing both."

That was the big difference between those two. Prudhomme wanted only to win, and McEwen always wanted to generate revenue so he could win.

RANDY FISH

FROM FAN TO FRIEND

Author's note: Both Tom McEwen and Don Prudhomme have depended on their relationship with the press to garner good exposure for their sponsors and their careers. Not only is Randy Fish the current editor of **Drag Racer** magazine, he is a true student of the sport of drag racing.

Having read every car magazine available from about 1960, it was probably those great radio ads on AM radio station WDRC that got my attention. Yeah, they were your typical "Sunday, Sunday, Sunday" spots, all exciting and each one of them ending with the words "Left on Buckley Hill Road, to … Connecticut Dragway!"

I continued to read everything I could get my hands on that contained custom cars, hot rods, and drag racing, and my dad built me a workbench next to his where I assembled all the coolest model cars of the time. I imagined Southern California was like Disneyland on nitro.

Fast forward a few years, and I started going to the Gatornationals in 1972, since it was a great way to escape at least one week of those brutal Northeast winters. I still have an old photo of Don Prudhomme and the famed *Yellow Feather* rear-engine Top Fuel dragster taken in Gainesville, Florida. Shortly thereafter, Prudhomme switched to Funny Car, and the amazing Snake and Mongoose Hot Wheels show was on the road.

I don't need to tell you how many times or where I've seen McEwen and Prudhomme race. What I would like to emphasize here is that, thanks to my work as a photojournalist, I've gone from fan to friend—most importantly with Don "the Snake" Prudhomme and Tom "the Mongoo$e" McEwen—of many luminaries from the sport of drag racing. Now, all you have to do is get these two guys together, and it's best described as a verbal smack-down. The digs go back and forth on a continual basis, but it's obvious that it's just part of their game. They've been rivals for decades, so why stop now?

Oh yeah, the Snake is as cool as they come. At the track, he's always got his guard up, and he remains focused on both his race car and his persona. This cat's intense. But at the shop or at home, he's in his element, and "the game face" diminishes—somewhat. It's cool to see the Snake away from the national event hustle and bustle, where he's done a masterful job landscaping the beautiful home where he and Lynn enjoy a peaceful existence. A great deal of that downtime includes special time with their beloved menagerie of dogs. At the shop, the Snake takes care of day-to-day business but also maintains a lifelong stash of peripheral materials from his storied career, as well as restoring significant machines that he's piloted to record-breaking performances. The dogs are also there every day, along with his wife, daughter Donna, and a small staff.

And the Mongoose, you ask? Well, he marches to the beat of a different drummer. Tom still loves keeping up with all the latest drag racing insider news, but his life revolves around several other endeavors too. McEwen keeps busy wheeling and dealing in the advertising sales department at *Drag Racer* magazine while I fill all the white space he doesn't sell. Outside of those duties, the Mongoose is a partner in a successful quarter horse racing stable, has an interest in drag racing collectibles, and always looks out for the almighty buck. His gruff exterior is lined with a heart of gold, and the man is generous to a fault. Every Monday evening, Tom looks forward to what he calls "The Obese Club Gathering," comprising Frankie Baney, Jimmy Rossi, Mike Kuhl, Tom Prock, Mike Thermos, and various others who all converge on the restaurant of McEwen's choosing.

Granted, it doesn't happen every day, but a lifelong fan can become friends with some of the biggest names in drag racing. I have to be reminded, for example, who's the Snake and who's the editor, but I'm okay with that. After all, it's a long way from Connecticut Dragway to Southern California, but it truly is like Disneyland on nitro.

Above and right: Prudhomme, with sponsorship from Wynn Oil Company, took his own fuel dragster on tour, accompanied by his wife, Lynn, (shown at the NHRA Winternationals). The Snake admits that touring on your own is a tough way to make a living. **Prudhomme Collection/Alan Earman photo/ NHRA National Dragster**

CHAPTER 6

THE SNAKE VERSION

THE PRELUDE

Author's note: The following two chapters are from tape recordings made with the Snake at his home in the summer of 2008.

It has been nearly 45 years since mechanic Dave Sowins, Mickey Thompson, and I stood in the Lions drag strip staging area and watched a young, skinny kid take a shot down the asphalt in a Kent Fuller–built, fuel-injected Buick dragster once owned by Tommy Ivo. At the time, it was just another kid making another run. Now the kid is a legend, and it's his turn to tell the story of the sponsorship package that made him a household name.

The setting is the spacious patio area of his home near San Diego. Several overstuffed lounge chairs are arranged facing a large outdoor fireplace. The Snake is relaxed, with his wonderful wife, Lynn, seated in close proximity—to act as backup to any details he may have forgotten.

Most of those who know the Snake will freely state that Lynn is the guiding force behind the Prudhomme racing interests; she has always provided the stable environment he needed to become successful and move beyond the difficult years when the Snake was just a local racer. Warned by her parents not to get involved with a dragster driver, Don and Lynn married while still in their teens and have built a strong marriage, raised a daughter, and created a top-level racing team.

Also in attendance is the family dog patrol, carefully watching every move the intruder with the recording device makes. Sadly, the leader of the pack, a golden retriever named Senna (after Formula One world champion Ayrton Senna), passed away shortly after the interview.

If you were racing a fuel dragster out at San Fernando Drag Strip in the early 1960s, you would have shared a pit area with the team of Dave Zeuschel and Don Prudhomme running their Kent Fuller–built front-engine digger. The guy in the T-shirt is the late Tom McCoury, and the guy with his hands on his hips, "The Loner" Tony Nancy. **Harry Hibler Collection**

By observations made by many who expressed themselves in this book, it is easy to conclude that Don Prudhomme has always been known as a hard-nosed racer. He will readily admit that he never wanted to cut anyone slack, give a break or an inch to a competitor. He raced to win. If he hurt some feelings, bloodied a nose, or took an advantage, so be it. The years have mellowed the man in some ways; there is a toss of gray in his hair, he uses glasses to read the fine print, and he enjoys partaking in life's more sophisticated rewards. Away from the racetrack he shows signs he might have rolled off the throttle slightly. But as a race car owner, once the smell of nitro is present, he coils for a strike, and old habits emerge.

Despite his perceived mean side, Prudhomme possesses a quick wit, a love for art and architecture, a great sense of humor, and an extreme sense of loyalty to his friends. His best moments as a stand-up comic emerge when the Mongoose shows up for any event to which the two are invited—interaction between the Snake and the Mongoose is still a natural spectacle.

Those who were there will get the full impact of this photo. Don Prudhomme took the short-wheelbase, ex–Tommy Ivo, injected Buick dragster and stuffed in a blown Chrysler Hemi. The result was a beast that would bite you in a heartbeat, but the Snake says, "That old Ivo car went every way but straight."
Steve Reyes

MAN OF LEGEND

We were all a bunch of no-name racers from the streets of Los Angeles and the San Fernando Valley, running tracks around Southern California. Every week we would end up at Lions, Pomona, Riverside, the Pond [San Fernando], places like that. Drag racing was just getting popular with the kids, and fuel-burning dragsters were the big turn-on. Everybody liked the speed, the smell and noise. If you drove a dragster, man, you were cool.

I met McEwen at Lions Drag Strip, and we got to be friends. I don't know, we just seemed to click like some people do. They click. Everybody knows that I got the name Snake and that he countered with the Mongoose. He beat me a couple of times, and I liked his attitude; he had a smart mouth, and most of the time backed it up. He always hung out with a cool crowd. Lou Baney, Ed Pink, Gene Adams—guys who were cool. I didn't have many friends back then simply because I lived way out in the Valley, and most of the other racers hung out in Los Angeles or Long Beach. The second reason was that I worked at a real job sanding and painting cars. I only raced on weekends

Everybody knows the story. Joel Purcell started calling me Snake, and Ed Donovan talked McEwen into becoming the Mongoose. Then because we raced at Long Beach more often than any other track, the announcer started picking up on the name thing, and then there were a bunch of cartoons in the **Drag News** newspaper. It didn't take a genius to play the name game in a series of match races. Remember, this was the mid-'60s and nobody was getting paid much in drag racing, so us fuel dragster racers had to dig up ways to make a buck.

Match racing was one way that the promoters could create excitement in order to draw in crowds. The more people, the more money a promoter could afford to pay out to the match racers. Tommy Ivo was a big draw. So was Gary "Wildman" Gabelich. With the Snake and Mongoose they had a natural. The local radio DJs would play up the deal on rock 'n' roll stations: "Be there Saturday night for the Snake vs. Mongoose showdown. The action starts at sundown. The Snake strikes and the Mongoose bites at Lions Drag Strip, located on 223rd St. and Alameda Street. Be there!"

McEwen was the one who got the entire publicity thing going, and he was the one who promoted the whole name deal. To me it was a nickname, like "Skippy" or something. I just didn't care. But, Tom was always looking for a way to make a buck. He hated working.

For me, driving and winning was my motivation factor. While I ran the Greer, Black, and Prudhomme car, we had a record of 236 wins and 7 losses. I figured the name thing was just a way to put some cash in my pocket. If getting a snake painted on my helmet and blowing off someone with an ugly rat on his helmet meant $500 in my pocket, no problem. I'll do the job.

After the Greer, Black, and Prudhomme car, I went to drive for Roland Leong, and we kicked some butt, including winning the NHRA Nationals at Indianapolis in 1965 and the Winternationals at Pomona the same year. Then I went with Ed Pink and Lou Baney to drive the SOHC Ford Fuel dragster that later became the Shelby Super Snake Ford. A sideline to this story is the fact that McEwen was driving the SOHC Ford, and Pink and Baney fired him and hired me. He was so pissed that he built a Fuel dragster and chased me around the country looking for any chance to put me on the trailer. He's still mad. Just ask him.

In 1968 I got involved with the Wynn Oil Company [Wynn's Friction Proofing], and, for the first time in my career, I had enough money to build a car and take it on the road. Lynn and I packed up and headed east. The fact that I had won the U.S. Nationals gave me a reputation in the Midwest, so we started booking appearances and actually went into business on our own. With McEwen after me all the time, the Snake and Mongoose rivalry was really cooking. The fans were digging it, and some money started rolling. Several other California teams, Beebe and Mulligan, Ivo, the Frantic Four, and others, would book some of the same tracks. We would all travel together, stay at the same motels, hang out after the races, play pranks and practical jokes, and help each other if a problem arose. It was a real gypsy lifestyle.

> **"If getting a snake painted on my helmet and blowing off someone with an ugly rat on his helmet meant $500 in my pocket, no problem. I'll do the job."**

His first love was always Top Fuel dragsters, and the Snake was one of the best when driving one. In 1967, after Lou Baney and Ed Pink fired Tom McEwen as the driver of the Brand Ford SOHC Ford Fueler, they replaced the Mongoose with Prudhomme. Take a moment and just study the position of the driver sitting only 19 inches behind a nitro bomb. The boys earned their bones. **Steve Reyes**

The more **Drag News** and local newspapers and radio stations played up the Snake and Mongoose circus, the more the fans got into taking sides. At some tracks the fans would boo me and cheer him, and at others they hated the Mongoose and loved the Snake. In reality, Tom was better with the fans. He had a knack for playing the crowds. I was the villain most of the time, but I won more races.

At this point in the story, I'm not thinking about making anything out of Snake vs. Mongoose except appearance money and match racing. In fact, with my Wynn Oil program, I was thinking of making a major push to take advantage of my reputation and book more tracks, maybe some without the Mongoose.

Then, one day, I was working on my dragster at Keith Black Racing Engines when McEwen comes up and tells me about this idea, and he wants to go to lunch. He starts telling me that his kids (he had a couple of boys) loved these little Hot Wheels cars. I didn't have any kids at the time, and I didn't know anything about toys. In fact, to be truthful, I didn't care about toys.

Well, McEwen has this way about making you feel stupid if you don't listen to what he is telling you. His voice gets low, and he gives you a look like, "How can you not know what I'm talking about?" So, he continues, saying Mattel Toy Company is making these little Hot Wheels cars and he is thinking about an idea of using the Snake and Mongoose rivalry to promote toy cars. I listened, but I was pretty happy with my Wynn Oil deal. They were paying me about seven grand a year, and, back in the late '50s, that was big money.

He doesn't stop. His mother is married to a lawyer (McEwen's stepdad) who does some work with Mattel, and she may be able to set up a meeting. I said, "Fine, go just to check things out." But I sort of shined the whole idea on.

A couple of weeks later, Tom comes back over to Black's shop and tells me, "Hey, Mattel likes the idea and they want to talk to us."

Dressed in a pair of bell-bottom pants, a clean shirt, and a sports coat I hadn't worn in a while, we head to Mattel in Redondo

Opposite and below: Once the Snake learned to love funny cars, he became a terror in the class. One of his most successful efforts was the Pontiac-bodied **Pepsi Challenger**. Prudhomme became more famous as a driver in the Funny Car class; he won the NHRA Funny Championship four times as a driver and two times as a car owner. **Steve Reyes**

Even more so than during their early careers as Southern California drag racers, the Snake and the Mongoose were always the center of attraction for the media during their national sponsorship from Mattel Toy Company. This was especially true at big events like the NHRA Supernationals at Ontario, California, where Steve Evans and Bill Fleming of ABC **Wide World of Sports** prepare to talk to Prudhomme.
Ed Justice Jr.

The reactions of the kids to the Mattel Hot Wheels program were the most rewarding. When asked about the program, Lynn Prudhomme said, "Both Don and Tom loved playing with the kids. And the kids had their favorites, and that became a constant arguing point between the two."
Prudhomme Collection

Beach. They love the idea! In fact, their art department and designers already have sketches of the cars. The problem for me is that the drawings are funny cars. Tom had been running a funny car off and on, but not me. I was a hardcore Fuel dragster driver. I wanted the fastest and quickest car. In my eyes the funny cars were a new gimmick to lure fans. Top Fuel was king of the sport, and I wasn't about to run second best. I didn't see myself running anything but a Fuel dragster.

Mattel insisted. McEwen was on my ass, and there was money to be made. I felt like an actor trying out for a starring role in some blockbuster movie and getting the part instantly, then having second thoughts. I was a bit confused, but I agreed.

At first I didn't like the paint scheme. It looked like a giant decal. Come to find out the paint design was created to make the decals for the production of the toys. Mattel was ready to go into production as fast as possible.

I still had no idea of what a big deal making little cars was going to be. Tom took the lead. We ordered two funny cars to be built by Ronnie Scrima, and it was decided that we should form a corporation. Actually, Mattel wouldn't seal the deal until

we incorporated. McEwen came up with the name Wildlife Racing Corporation, and my wife, Lynn, and Tom's mom, Sybil, put together the fine print. Tom's mom worked for the same high-powered law firm (Ball, Hunt, Hart, and Brown) as his stepdad, so she was a key player in the whole program.

The way it came together, Tom and I were partners and directors, my wife was manager, and Tom's mom was treasurer. To put the icing on the cake, Tom got involved with a local marketing company that was handling big names like Mario and the Unser brothers. The reason, according to Tom's thinking, was the marketing company could approach other companies to get onboard the Mattel deal and put their logos on the cars. Oh man, was that a match made in heaven. I said to myself, "Oh baby, this is getting interesting."

Along with the Mattel sponsorship package, we added Chrysler/Plymouth Division [the cars were a Duster and a Barracuda, both with Hemi engines], Goodyear, Coca-Cola, Wynn Oil, Cragar, Federal Mogul, Pennzoil, plus all of the parts manufacturers. I have heard all kinds of numbers dealing with the contracts we made, but after having Lynn look up some of the old records I can give you a rough, very rough, idea of what we got.

According to what we could piece together, the initial Mattel contract gave us about 30 grand apiece per year. The other major sponsors kicked in anywhere from $16,000 from Coca-Cola to $25,000 from Chrysler/Plymouth. The rest ranged from 5 grand and up. The money was split 50/50, and we had to pay our expenses. The thing that helped with expenses was the appearance money we got from track owners. The bottom line was that it was a bunch of money for two drag racers from Southern California. We did not get royalties on the toys until Mattel became an associate sponsor. And, one little known fact: somebody produced a TV cartoon show for kids featuring the Snake and Mongoose. For allowing them to use our name we got a residual deal.

Looking back, maybe we could have made better long-term deals, but I wasn't thinking of anything but racing, and, in 1970, a hundred grand was more money than I figured I could spend. You can ask Lynn. I was a bad promoter and a worse businessman.

At first, all of the money went into a pot at Wildlife Racing, and we could each pull out what we wanted. Quick enough our

Above and opposite: Today, Don "the Snake" Prudhomme is a car owner and has given up the driver chores to a young hot shoe named Spencer Massey. But, in his time, Don Prudhomme was one of the most feared drivers in all of drag racing, and he became a Funny Car legend. Shown here are two of his most famous cars, the **Pepsi Challenger** and the **Hot Wheels Plymouth**. Steve Reyes

Both Tom McEwen and Don Prudhomme made names in drag racing prior to the Mattel Toy program. Prudhomme gained great attention for his exploits in the Greer, Black, and Prudhomme Top Fuel dragster as well as the car shown here, built by Kent Fuller and powered by a Dave Zeuschel Chrysler. **Prudhomme Collection**

personalities showed up. Tom was the showman, and all this was his idea, so he wanted to keep up his image. I would spend $200 on a new supercharger, and he would spend $2,000 on chrome parts, fancy shoes, clothes, and a new watch. He liked the showman part of the deal. I was a penny pincher, and he was a flash dancer. So, after a short time, we decided to separate the account into his and mine. I can't remember every detail and every penny we made, but I can tell you straight up that the Mattel Toy Hot Wheels program was the first and biggest non-automotive sponsorship package in the history of drag racing.

THE KIDS-AND-TOYS FACTOR

Our first official program was at the Mattel Company headquarters, and all of the employees and press were on hand. We gave out the Hot Wheels Snake vs. Mongoose drag racing game. It was huge, very cool; everyone at Mattel was pumped. They were all more excited than I was. I was excited about the dough and the thought that we could make a living drag racing. But, I still didn't get the picture with the kids and the toys.

Once we got on the road, things really changed. We started match racing all over the country, and when we got to the Midwest I began to realize how much effort Mattel was putting into the program and how popular Hot Wheels toys were.

For example, let's say we were going to a typical Midwest town, like Milan, Michigan. Mattel would have their public relations and promotion team come in a few days early, set up a promotion with a toy store at a mall or shopping center, then ship in a supply of toys and games. The local newspapers and radio stations would advertise "Kids! Come and meet the real Snake and Mongoose, see their race cars up close, play the Mattel Hot Wheels game and win prizes. Bring Mom and Dad."

You couldn't believe the crowds. Man, it was nuts. All these little kids running around with a pocketful of Hot Wheels. Tom was better at mingling with the crowds. When we first started, I wanted to get the appearance thing over with and head for the track.

What happened was Hot Wheels became a fad throughout the whole country. You got to remember that this was before video games and computer games and kids growing up by the time they're 12 years old. Kids could be kids, and they liked to play cars. It was old-school stuff.

One great story that comes to mind happened during the filming of a video of our Hot Wheels tour sponsored by Coca-Cola. The film was called **Once upon a Wheel**, and it was part of a coupon program. When you bought a six-pack of Coca-Cola, you got a discount on Hot Wheels Snake and Mongoose cars.

Anyway, we pull into the track at Milan, Michigan, and it's raining like a cow peeing on a flat rock. Tom and I are sitting in the tow truck, and the camera is running, and we're making small talk. These boys run up to the truck, and McEwen says, "Hey, you got any Hot Wheels?" And the kids come back, "Yeah, we got Snake and Mongoose." McEwen says, "Who's the fastest?" The boys yell, "Snake!"

He was so pissed. I'll never forget, he looks hard at me and says, "You paid those kids to say that." It was priceless.

THE BETTER HALF

[Author's note: Lynn Prudhomme offers her take on the early days with Mattel.]

Both Tom and Don really love kids. They were both natural playmates for the kids, and they picked up on that from the beginning. There was nothing phony. Mattel would even have the boys come to the company toy test sessions, and they would bring in a bunch of kids and turn them loose to play and react to the newest Hot Wheels. Before you knew it, Don and Tom were on the floor, playing with the kids.

Remember the Chevy Monza? While many Monza owners would eventually want to set their cars on fire, that's not what the Snake is doing here. This is a "fire burnout." Although regular pre-race burnouts help heat and clean the tires, the only purpose fire burnouts serve is to impress the fans in the stands. Popular for a few years, fire burnouts were eventually banned by the NHRA for being too dangerous.

BOB SHAFFER

Author's note: From 1974 to 1980, one of Goodyear Tire and Rubber Company's sales and marketing representative positions was held by a man named Bob Shaffer. Bob was involved in NHRA drag racing, and his responsibility was to promote the use of Goodyear drag racing tires. At the time, Goodyear was in a heated competition with the M&H Racemaster tire created by Marv Rifchin. Shaffer was thrown into the battle without much warning of what to expect. He would become close friends with both Don Prudhomme and Tom McEwen.

When I started in 1974, most of the top dogs in Fuel dragsters were running M&H Racemaster slicks because they worked very well on all types of tracks. It was basically the same story in Funny Cars; the guys liked M&H and were not eager to switch. Finally, we convinced both Don Garlits and Gary Beck to join our team. My task, then, was to make further gains in Top Fuel and Funny Car by demonstrating that Goodyear tires could compete. My first race was the 1975 NHRA Winternationals at Pomona, California. It was very exciting because I had been a drag racing fan for years, and, although you didn't see much drag racing on TV, when I was a kid we all read every magazine on the newsstand. I had also owned a Snake vs. Mongoose Hot Wheels drag racing game, so I looked forward to meeting all of the drivers up close and personal.

At that first race, Tom McEwen came driving up to our Goodyear exhibit in a big Cadillac coupe and introduced himself. The first words out of his mouth were a request. He wanted to know if he could get some free tires for his hauler. I said, "No, I'm not giving you any truck tires, it's not part of my job." He snapped back, "Well, that's it; I'm pulling Goodyear off my car and running M&H tires, they work better anyway."

The reality was that both Tom and Don had run Goodyear tires and M&H tires, switching back and forth depending which tire worked best. Back in those days, there were no big binding contracts; most of the deals came with a handshake. In fact, some teams bought their own tires—no deals from a manufacturer.

As time went by, Goodyear began a serious effort to put its tire in the spotlight. In 1976, Goodyear introduced a new drag slick—16 1/2 inches wide, a 34-1/2-inch OD, and a 110-inch rollout. Don Garlits tried a set, and they worked very well. Next, Raymond Beadle started running the tire on his Blue Max funny car. But Garlits and Beadle were only two out of many, and we wanted to expand the number of teams using the new Goodyear drag slick. I forget the track, but McEwen came up to me and wanted to try a set of our new tires. I was still upset with him for leaving us and going to M&H, so I said, "Well I'm not going to give them to you but you can buy a set at the racer price." Oh man, McEwen didn't like that ultimatum at all, and to this day he swears those were the only tires he ever bought.

Tom liked the tires, and from that point on we made a deal to supply him with tires. Back then, not much money ever changed hands, but if one of our teams got in trouble we would help. I remember one time when McEwen's crew crashed the tow rig and it caught fire. The result cost Tom a ton of money, so the next time I saw him at the track I bought him a 55-gallon of nitro just to help out.

As for Prudhomme, he was a hard case, and I never figured I could talk him out of running M&H tires, so I didn't really try. Then, at the NHRA Molson Grandnational in Montreal, Canada, I was having breakfast in the hotel, and the Snake came wandering in. I said, "Snake, what's going on?" And, in his too-cool Steve McQueen low mumble he said, "Hey Bob, I really need to try a set of those new tires." We agreed, and in 1979 at the NHRA Nationals, Don set the ET record for Funny Cars, becoming the first ever to run in the 5-second bracket (5.95).

Once we got Prudhomme to switch, the floodgates opened, and everyone wanted to use the new Goodyear tire.

In retrospect, I have been involved in racing since 1967, and I can say without hesitation that, when the funny cars came to drag racing, including the Snake vs. Mongoose Hot Wheels rivalry, it was a turning point in the sport's history. The funny cars brought a new dimension to the sport. The fans loved the names: Chi-Town Hustler, Blue Max, Jungle Jim, the Hawaiian, Trojan Horse, Omar "the Tentmaker" Carruthers, Strip

around racing I have seen many drivers come and go—the superstars and the also-ran nobodies. But, my favorite of the bunch is the Mongoose.

Yeah, Prudhomme did more winning, but once I got to know Tom and got past his public image, we became friends, and I just learned to like his racing style. I found that the sarcastic remarks, his always trying to one-up Prudhomme, were his public face, his act. Under it all he would give a friend the shirt off his back.

As for the Snake, during his career as a driver, Prudhomme was one of the most competitive, intense, serious racers I ever met. In my career, only Don Garlits is in the same league. Off the track, Prudhomme was always a shy and reclusive guy who considered friendship a serious matter and something that had to be earned.

The bottom line is that both guys were a driving force in the growth of drag racing, especially when it came to bringing the sport to the attention of corporate America.

I forget the track, but McEwen came up to me and wanted to try a set of our new tires. I was still upset with him for leaving us and going to M&H, so I said, "Well I'm not going to give them to you but you can buy a set at the racer price." Oh man, McEwen didn't like that ultimatum at all, and to this day he swears those were the only tires he ever bought.

Blazer, Budweiser King, Snake and Mongoose, and the list goes on. The cars looked like real cars, and then there was the ritual of the drivers getting ready: flipping up the top and lighting the engine, the awesome burnouts, the particular noise only created by a nitro-burning funny car, it all joined as one super sensation for the senses. And, the racing was unreal—wheel stands, cars sideways at 200 miles per hour, blower explosions, body liftoffs, and side-by-side racing that would put the fans in a state of hallucination. The Snake and Mongoose helped foster those images. Even today, at my age, the hair on the back of my neck stands up when I think about funny cars in the 1970s.

As for the personal side of Prudhomme and McEwen, I have an opinion or two. In the 40 years I have been

Certainly, both the Snake and the Mongoose had a strong influence in putting Goodyear Tire Company on the map in drag racing. Speaking as the guy who worked closely with Don and Tom when they were under contract to Goodyear, I can relate one point that tells their story, something that few outside of drag racing will ever read.

When we would hire a team for testing Goodyear drag slicks, part of the deal was that we would pay for any breakage. Many times, teams would come out with junk engines, would blow up, and then would have Goodyear replace the parts with new top-of-the-line equipment. Neither the Snake nor the Mongoose ever pulled that crap. They would run as hard as they could with their best equipment so Goodyear would get the most accurate data. That type of integrity is what made them stars.

For the first season of the Mattel Hot Wheels program, both Tom and Don ran what could be called the transitional-type funny car. The chassis had coil springs, a very short wheelbase, and a two-speed B&M automatic transmission. **Ed Justice Jr.**

CHAPTER 7

THE END OF THE RUN

ON THE FIX

Author's note: As it had been with the Mongoose, the answer to the question of whether they played favorites when setting up match races was unequivocal. In fact, the Snake's response was even more animated than that of the Mongoose. The Snake reacted by throwing his arms in the air and producing a loud laugh.

Oh my god, are you kidding me? I wanted to beat him like a circus monkey every time we came to the starting line. I wanted to win every race. And our crews felt the same way. His guys wanted to kick ass on my guys as bad as he wanted to beat me. I remember getting so mad when McEwen would beat me that I wouldn't talk to him for a week.

Then I would realize that I was being a punk and that we still had to go down the road together and promote Hot Wheels. So I would give in, but it didn't lessen the idea that I hated getting beat. There were times when Tom and I had to pull the crews apart because the two of us had ragged on each other so bad that our crew guys would get pissed. We never fixed a race, and I ran him as hard as I could. No way could I back off. That's why I won so many races.

THE SCENE

[Author's note: As for the conditions presented by some of the more obscure race tracks the Hot Wheels team had to compete on, the Snake had a rather obtuse view of the circumstances.]

We, or at least I, didn't give a crap about any of the tracks. Man, I didn't care if they were long, short, wide, or narrow. I would send my guys down to the far end with a half-dozen fire extinguishers and tell them, "Let's race." We would make

a run, and the guys would haul butt in the push car to get to me if I had it to a stop.

And, speaking of push cars, we used to borrow push cars from the fans at the track. Before a race, I would go around and yell, "Hey, man, can we use your car to chase the race car?" They would yell back, "Yeah man, whatever you need." We would load all our tools and stuff in a stranger's car and go up to the starting line to make a pass. By the end of the day or night, the car would be out of gas, covered in tire dust and empty soda cans. But the owners didn't care. They wanted to be part of the action.

There were times when fans would come out of the grandstands and help us get the cars ready. They would be happy doing little stuff like holding the lines when we were packing the chutes or chasing down lunch for my guys. Several times I have asked fans to go into a local town and pick up parts or take a piece to a buddy of theirs who had a welding shop or machine shop. It was cool, getting the fans involved. Even today, some guy will come up to me at the races and say, "You know, I remember meeting you in 1970 when you had the Hot Wheels car and you let me hand you oil cans while you were changing oil."

Within a year or so, we got to be a big deal around the country. My head got a little tight for my helmet. But, I was on top of the world, my small world. I remember being at the Indy 500, and I was walking around in Gasoline Alley when I pass the garage used by

Here is a rather unusual photo of the Snake doing something other than driving a fuel-burning race car. In this case he is acting as a color commentator for NBC at the Sand Drags. Prudhomme is talking to Al Westfall, driver of a blown fuel Jeep sand funny car. Good thing the Snake stuck with his day job. **Steve Reyes**

For several seasons after the Hot Wheels program moved on, Prudhomme maintained a great relationship with Mattel and ran both a Funny Car entry and a Top Fuel dragster, always carrying the Hot Wheels logo somewhere on the car. **Prudhomme Collection**

Mario Andretti. I look in, and Mario is talking to his mechanic, a man named Clint Brawner, when he turns and says, "Hey Snake, come on in." I was so pumped to be recognized by Mario Andretti. He was a god back then, and he was calling me. How cool is that?

PRIORITIES

[Author's note: When choosing between running NHRA National events and running their scheduled Mattel booking dates and match races, the Snake showed his realistic way of looking at things.]

For us, the NHRA National events were not that important. There weren't as many as today, and our main focus was to show off the Hot Wheels program and meet our obligations to track owners who booked us in for match races. Another reason we didn't like National events was the fact that during the first year of the program our cars were not on a par with the latest and greatest stuff running. We had automatic transmissions, coil-spring

suspension systems, and short-wheelbase chassis. It was like driving a Super Stock car on nitro.

My big deal at the NHRA Nationals was to run my dragster along with the Hot Wheels funny car. I even had Butch Maas drive the funny car while I ran my digger at one of the Nationals. Later, I converted my Don Long–chassis dragster into my half of the program when Mattel wanted us to run a dragster with the funny car.

When Mattel came out with a game called the Mongoose & Snake Wild Wheelie Set, their designers came up with a dragster body that had a side-board effect. They were way different than the other dragsters on the scene, but it was Mattel's idea, and they were paying the bills. The good news was that at the same time period we started running new funny cars built by John Buttera, and the difference was amazing. The cars worked like a real race car— they handled and went straight. The roll cage was better, the whole car was state-of-the-art, and from that point I was hooked on funny cars. The [Mattel] dragsters only lasted about a year.

Throughout the three-year Hot Wheels program, the Mattel Toy Company placed very few restrictions on the Snake and the Mongoose. During their wild odyssey, they featured many styles and colors on their cars, including the dreaded all-black **Snake III** run by Prudhomme in late 1972. Interesting trivia: These two cars made the last run at Lions Drag Strip before it closed. **Steve Reyes**

Left and below: For one year after Mattel Toy Company went from full sponsorship to associate sponsorship, Tom McEwen and Don Prudhomme promoted the Beech Nut Company and their Care Free gum products as a major sponsor. The program just didn't work out.
Steve Reyes

One of the emotional road blocks presented by spending a good portion of your life on the road is being separated from your family. Here Don shares a few moments with his daughter Donna. **Prudhomme Collection/Les Lovett**

Left: Driving a fuel-burning funny car can get a little shaky sometimes. This was the debut run for the Snake's 1971 Hot Wheels–sponsored car at Scottsdale, Arizona. It replaced his original yellow car from 1970. **Steve Reyes**

Below: At the conclusion of the Mattel program, Snake and Mongoose moved on to explore different options. McEwen picked up a deal with the Navy, and Prudhomme picked up the Army. **Steve Reyes**

Above and right: When Mattel became an associate sponsor on all the cars both McEwen and Prudhomme ran, the Snake moved back to his roots, running several versions of a rear-engine Top Fuel dragster. The wedge car (right) was not very successful, but a lightweight car, dubbed by Don Garlits the **Yellow Feather** because of its minimalism, worked great. **Steve Reyes**

MATTEL MOVES ON

[Author's note: The period of time that began the day Tom McEwen walked into the offices of Mattel Toy Company and lasted until the Hot Wheels program began to fade into the history books encompasses about three years. By 1973, Mattel had changed their position from full sponsor of Tom McEwen and Don Prudhomme to associate sponsor and had set up a royalty program with the Snake and the Mongoose on the sale of toys. Prudhomme talked about how one of the greatest programs ever to play a role in the sport of drag racing ended its run.]

I think it was about three years before the original craze for Snake and Mongoose toys had cooled and Mattel was moving in different directions. We kept a great relationship with the company, and they stayed with us as an associate. In fact, we are still involved with Mattel on various levels. Throughout the years they have been like family to us, and we never forget the opportunity they gave us.

But McEwen, never one to pass up the likelihood of making a buck, concocted a deal with Beechnut Gum company to promote Care Free sugarless gum. He was going to be one flavor, and I would be another. The deal lasted about a year, if that. I had enough of a reputation that I didn't have trouble putting together programs. We had a super deal with the Army, and I switched from the Plymouth Barracuda body to a Chevy Monza. Some of the associate sponsors stayed with me, and I don't think the Mattel Hot Wheels idea and the Snake vs. Mongoose thing ever stopped in the minds of the fans.

Getting back to the Hot Wheels thing, I got to get something straight about the Snake vs. Mongoose rivalry. You know, everybody thinks that Tom and I didn't get along or that we never worked together, but that is about as far from the truth as you can get. When Tom and I ran the NHRA National events, all of the hot shoe funny car teams from around the country would show up— Jungle Jim, Blue Max, the Chi-Town Hustler, Mickey Thompson—and

"You know, everybody thinks that Tom and I didn't get along or that we never worked together, but that is about as far from the truth as you can get."

every one of them wanted a piece of us. I think there was a little sour grapes about the Mattel deal and the fact that we had been the first to put together a promotion package like Hot Wheels, so beating us was a chance to do a little nose-rubbing in the dirt.

So, if Tom felt like I was getting jumped on too hard, he would pitch in and offer whatever I needed. We would talk setup, track conditions, and tires. In fact, we were running at Bristol, Tennessee, one year, and I was under contract to Goodyear. At this race we had both the funny cars and I had my dragster. I went to Tom and told him that the Goodyear tires weren't working for me and asked for help. Tom was a close friend of Marv Rifchin of M&H. So, Tom got Marv to put on a set of M&H tires, and I won the event. Back in the day, Goodyear wouldn't hold you to your contract if their tires didn't work. In today's world, the lawyers would be at your throat in an instant.

Tom was always ready to help if I needed it. All that talking smack was just our act.

The other issue that needs clearing up is the idea of who won the most races. I was lucky and won the majority of the races we ran. I just worked harder and wanted it more. Tom raced just as hard, but he liked other things in life. To me, winning was the only thing, and that issue caused more problems than any other. At times I wasn't fair to Tom. I would get pissed if he won but expected him to accept my winning without comment. In the end Tom was OK with me winning. He would just make a joke or two and go on with his life.

The bottom line to this story is that the Mattel Hot Wheels deal turned my career around in a big way. If it had not been for the ideas and vision Tom came up with, who knows what could or would have happened. The money we made and the contacts we developed helped both of us become stars in the sport of drag racing.

I owe a lot to McEwen, but I don't tell him. Instead, I tell him that I got so used to beating him that it made beating the other teams easier because I had so much practice.

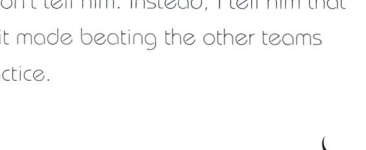

"WATERBED" FRED MILLER

Author's note: He once bought a waterbed for five dollars, and it leaked. The name stuck. Drag racers are a tough crowd to hang with.

Everybody knows me as "Waterbed"; it is a nickname given to me by Dale Emery. My introduction into drag racing came when I was living in Ohio and went to work for Bob Riggle when he was running the Hemi under Glass wheel-stander. Later I moved on to a funny car as part of the crew on the old Don Gay Pontiac funny car. The experience I gained by working on a full-fledged fuel funny car eventually led to my joining the crew of the Blue Max funny car.

I need to clarify the time period on my involvement on the Blue Max team. The Blue Max funny car actually began when Harry Schmidt introduced the first version in the late 1960s with various drivers, most notably wild men Richard Tharp and Jake Johnson. Then the Max went into hibernation for a time, then returned with Harry owning the car and Raymond Beadle driving. It was during this period I joined the fray with crew chief Dale Emery.

But, before my involvement with the Max, I had my first encounter with the Snake and Mongoose. On December 2, 1972, I attended the "Last Drag Race" at the closing of Lions Drag Strip in Long Beach, California. It was kind of weird. I had read about the Snake and Mongoose, seen the Hot Wheels toys, and heard all of the stories. But until you come to a place like Long Beach and you see them up close and personal, it doesn't have the same meaning.

The fact that it was the last drag race at Long Beach made everything going on that night even more bizarre; crowds had broken down the fences, there were 20,000 people in a place that should hold no more than 10,000, and, to quote from an article in the February 1973 issue of *Hot Rod* magazine, "The pungent odor of marijuana hung heavy over the track, overpowering even the nitro fumes belching from the staged Funny Cars." I never got to actually meet either of them, but they put on a show to end all shows. McEwen and Prudhomme came to do battle in the Funny Car final. Two Hot Wheels cars facing off, the Snake vs. the Mongoose, what a scene. McEwen won, and, as the saying goes, the crowd went wild.

My actually becoming friends with McEwen and Prudhomme occurred when I was crewing on a Funny Car Camaro owned by Jeg Coughlin and driven by Dale Emery. During our West Coast swing, we kept the car at Ed Pink Racing Engines. Prudhomme kept his car in a shop located in the same complex, so I got to know him and his crew chief Bob Brandt. Ed Pink was also close friends with McEwen, so it was natural that I got to know Tom. But, my story is not one of being a team member or crewmember with either Prudhomme or McEwen, my view of them comes from being a competitor, an outsider who was one of those trying to beat them and to gather up some of the fame and fortune being created by the funny car rage. As I mentioned, I ended up as a crewmember on the Blue Max car with Raymond Beadle, and we became part of the funny car explosion. Beginning in the early 1970s, funny cars took over drag racing.

If you knew Raymond Beadle, then you would know that on the track he was a ferocious competitor, but, when not racing, the Blue Max crew, myself included, hung out with Prudhomme and McEwen. We all traveled down the road together. Back in those days, the race crews were small, and nearly everyone traveled in makeshift convoys from track to track.

For some reason, Prudhomme and I got along, which was unusual because Don didn't hang out with many people. He was very intense, hated losing more than Beadle, and at the track he was as serious as a heart attack. Prudhomme wouldn't let anyone in his pit during a race. He would run sponsors out; the guy was hardcore, and for some reason I liked the way he raced.

On the other hand, everyone got along with the Mongoose. It was hilarious, watching the two Hot Wheels stars do their act. McEwen was always promoting something; selling T-shirts, selling hats, taking pictures with the fans—especially any and all good-looking girls—and playing with the kids. The Snake would work

other would make the final round of eliminations. But, the really big deal was when they would meet in a final. Actually, McEwen was a very good driver, and I can tell you point blank that they never fixed a race. They both ran flat-out, no favors.

It was interesting to watch the two personalities in action. Both guys would fight through the other competition and then end up meeting in the final. If

Back in those days, the race crews were small, and nearly everyone traveled in makeshift convoys from track to track.

and study, then work more. No two teammates were ever more different.

At the peak of the funny car phenomenon, match racing and buy-ins were how the teams made money. Track promoters would book in all the name cars: the Chi-Town Hustler, Jungle Jim, the Blue Max, the Snowman, Shirley Muldowney, the Strip Blazer, the Hawaiian, and Snake vs. Mongoose. Just to make things interesting, local cars would come out and try and take out the names. If a promoter could book in an eight-car show of big names plus locals, he had a moneymaker. Most teams would run as many match races or pay races as possible. We would only run NHRA National events to get publicity for the sponsors and to get ink in the magazines. The more press, the more appearance money.

Prudhomme and McEwen always had good equipment, and they had a very cool act. Most of the time, one or the

McEwen won, he was not the type to blow his own horn. He was just a good sport. But, if Prudhomme got beat, he would get so pissed off that he wouldn't talk to McEwen for a week.

The truth of the matter was, Prudhomme was the guy to beat during the 1970s, and Raymond wanted to knock him off the top worse than anything. Finally, in 1979, the Blue Max took the Funny Car title away from the Snake, and, for me, that was a big deal because, friends or not, we wanted to win.

In closing, you can say whatever you want about Snake and Mongoose, but the reality is that McEwen and Prudhomme took Funny Car racing in particular and drag racing in general to a higher level. After the Hot Wheels deal with Mattel, it was easier for everyone who was looking for sponsorship money to make a presentation. I say, thank God for McEwen and his vision and slick talking.

This Hot Wheels promotional poster captures the way the Snake vs. Mongoose rivalry transcended the traditional drag racing scene and moved into mainstream 1970s pop culture. **McEwen collection**

CHAPTER 8
THE RIVALRY THAT CHANGED A GENERATION

Author's note: With the Hot Wheels story already told by both the Snake and the Mongoose, there was still something lacking. Then it struck me: We had not heard from the manufacturer. I needed to get the inside angle on how a toy company had hooked up with two young California racers and created one of the most successful alliances in toy, and racing, history.

In reality, Mattel never anticipated the response from the public when it came to the introduction of the Hot Wheels line, but, very quickly, signs were obvious that the company had a hit toy on their hands. Kids began collecting and trading the cars and started buying them as fast as they could save their allowances. It was only common sense—if you were a kid, you would want Hot Wheels. They were cool, they were collectible, and they fit in your pocket.

It seems that the stars were aligned and the timing was perfect when Tom McEwen came wandering into the inner sanctum of Mattel Toy Company with an idea for a racing sponsorship. From Mattel's point of view, the Snake vs. Mongoose sponsorship package was the company's way of getting the toys out to the kids around the country. At first it was just a racing promotion, but within a very short time it became much more.

The concept was like magic—everything that could go perfectly did.

To get the Hot Wheels story from the Mattel side, I gathered a consensus from three individual sources: Chris Bouman, current senior manager of marketing for Mattel Toy Company; Larry Wood, one of the original designers of the Snake and Mongoose Hot Wheels cars; and Jerry Frye (pronounced Fire), director of product planning at the time of the Snake vs. Mongoose program.

CHRIS BOUMAN

Mattel Toy Company, founded by Elliot and Ruth Handler, had become famous with its Barbie doll series, but company execs were constantly looking for that next Big Idea. With that in mind, Elliot and several company designers, including Harry Bradley, created the first Hot Wheels cars sometime in 1968. At a meeting where the prototype for the first cars was shown, Elliot rolled the tiny model across the table, and a remark was made that those were some "hot wheels," and a toy legend was born.

At the time, the original Hot Wheels cars were based on the California look and feel. It was the custom look; California, especially Southern California, was notorious for wild customs (George Barris and Dean Jefferies made wild customs famous in the movies), outrageous hop-ups, and street racing. The first line of Hot Wheels emphasized speed and wild designs. In fact, the original lineup of 16 models all had red lines on the tires to indicate hot wheels.

The Snake and Mongoose competition, in the form of match racing at local drag strips around the country, started a buzz with the kids. The excitement was picked up in magazines and in newspapers, and the rivalry grew more popular at every event. The kids all wanted to be like the Snake and the Mongoose, but in order to play the part they had to have a Hot Wheels car.

The Hot Wheels concept has always been about excess, and the idea for the types of cars Tom McEwen and Don Prudhomme raced was the ultimate in excess.

125

Mattel celebrated its 35th Hot Wheels Snake and Mongoose Anniversary with a festive dinner and reception in July 2005. Tom McEwen's Hot Wheels Duster was re-created for the exciting evening, while Don Prudhomme restored his original Hot Wheels 'Cuda. Mattel recently re-released two Hot Wheels toys based on the cars (inset). **Don Prudhomme Collection/Mattel, Inc.**

LARRY WOOD

[Author's note: Although the original Hot Wheels toy car designs came about due to the vision of Mattel founder Elliot Handler, Harry Bradley, and several in-house designers, a young hot rodder, self-proclaimed car nut, and designer named Larry Wood was responsible for developing the prototype race cars to be used in the Snake vs. Mongoose program. Although it had been decided by Mattel designers and management from the beginning that the Snake and the Mongoose would use funny cars, the final composition of the race cars was not determined until later.

Now retired but still active in car design and the invention of new products, Larry Wood offers his insight into the early days of the program.]

By the time I got involved with the program, Mattel had decided that the Hot Wheels cars would be funny cars. In the late 1960s and early 1970s, funny cars had just exploded onto the drag racing scene, and everybody was going nuts over them. Also, they offered more space for logos and sponsor names.

Actually, I was a drag race freak and spent many Saturday nights at Long Beach. It was because of my being a car nut that I got the job at Mattel. Back then, I was working at Lockheed Aircraft, and at a party one night I met a guy who was a Hot Wheels designer at Mattel, and he was telling me that he really didn't want to be designing little toy cars. So, I applied and got the job. It was simply coincidence that my employment began at the same time as the Snake and Mongoose program began.

My first assignment was to go out to the Don Prudhomme race shop and start taking measurements of the chassis and body. Next came my design drawings and then actual engineering drawings and finally everything went to the pattern makers. Back then, there were no CAD-CAM engineering and design programs on a computer; they still made patterns from wood and then poured the die-cast models.

I can't remember who actually designed the graphics on the real cars, but I did them for the toys.

Rumor around the company was that Hot Wheels would be a flash in the pan and after six months they would drop the line. But,

by the time Snake vs. Mongoose was introduced, it was apparent that Mattel had hit on something special.

[Author's note: Larry Wood stayed on the Snake and Mongoose program, developing various versions of the Snake and Mongoose game sets including the *Wild Wheelie* dragsters featuring the deployment of tiny parachutes at the finish line. He confirmed that there was a prototype *Wild Wheelie* funny car, but it was never put into production.

Larry Wood stayed with the Mattel Toy Company for 40 years and has remained a car enthusiast throughout. Among Hot Wheels collectors, Wood is a hero, the man behind the Snake and Mongoose toy creation.]

The Mattel Hot Wheels program expanded in its second year to include fuel dragsters. The cars became the real-life models for a Hot Wheels set (designed by Larry Wood) called the **Mongoose & Snake Wild Wheelie Set**. The two dragsters were actually constructed from chassis Prudhomme and McEwen already owned. **Steve Reyes**

JERRY FRYE

[Author's note: One of the original members of the Mattel Toy Company management group during the Snake vs. Mongoose program, Jerry Frye was director of product planning for the company.]

When Tom McEwen came to Mattel, I was director of product planning, which was the group responsible for putting together product lines from ideas that came from our own in-house designers or from ideas coming from the outside world. At the time, we were getting about 3,000 proposals per year, with 99 percent rejected from the beginning, so Tom had a pretty steep hill to climb.

Actually, the Hot Wheels line of die-cast cars had blossomed into a very successful product. What could be simpler: clamp a looping 18-foot piece of yellow extruded plastic track onto a chair or table and let two tiny cars race. As far as our department was concerned, Hot Wheels cars were the biggest deal to hit the boy's toy market. Mattel was doing millions in sales. It was not up to the level of Barbie, but it was growing very quickly.

I'm not sure that everyone knows Mattel was involved with several racing efforts or teams during the late 1960s and early 1970s. Dan Gurney, Swede Savage in the Trans-Am series, Bruce McLaren in the Can-Am series, and Bob Unser at Indianapolis. But, all of those efforts involved individual teams or drivers; they did not compete with other Hot Wheels–sponsored cars. In fact, in the case of Bruce McLaren, the Can-Am series was not very popular with small kids. I think that the same held true of the others. Kids bought the cars because they looked cool and, in some cases, [because] their dads were fans.

The most appealing point to the Tom McEwen proposal was twofold: kids were more into drag racing, and the Snake and Mongoose were in the same class of racing and both carried the Hot Wheels logo. An added bonus was the fact that the snake and the mongoose were real and natural enemies, so there was a built-in competition from the start. You could almost see the handwriting on the wall from the beginning—Snake and Mongoose was going to be a hit.

"You could almost see the handwriting on the wall from the beginning—Snake and Mongoose was going to be a hit."

On a personal level, it was a fun time working with those two, especially during the contract negotiations; the bickering and haggling was nonstop as to who got top billing, who got the most money, and all the rest. I learned later that they had been doing that act for years. The boys took their alter ego rivalry seriously.

Back in those days, the most powerful form of advertising was TV; the cartoon shows in the mornings and on Saturday were a major path for the promotion of Mattel toys.

However, this is not to say we didn't explore other avenues. My department, myself included, would attend most of the major races, and we would bring our displays of the games and offer the race fans promotional material so they could buy the toys at a local dealer. We did not sell the sets at the races. Another great sales tool became our local distributors around the country. On a local level, distributors would work with the Mattel Sales Promotion Department to set up appearances at local malls, shopping centers, and toy stores. The combination of all the various departments working together produced a very well-rounded program, and this was the primary reason the Snake vs. Mongoose game sets sold so well.

It was a program that was great for kids. There was a friendly rivalry with great characters with fun names. But, the key to success became the fact that the kids could buy both figures and race them together under the same name, "Mattel Hot Wheels." Kids are naturally competitive, so half wanted to be the Snake and the other half the Mongoose. Unlike some of the games available today, everything about the Snake and Mongoose was positive. Neither was ever involved in a scandal or negative action. Their image fit well with our company image. On the plus side for the race team, the Hot Wheels program provided McEwen and Prudhomme more exposure than any other drag racing team, making them the most popular drag racing characters in the country.

On a personal level, it was a great joy to be a part of the Snake vs. Mongoose program and the rivalry it produced. For the fans, McEwen and Prudhomme were real heroes, and, because of the way drag racing was set up, they were accessible to the kids. Put real-life heroes together with kids and toys, and you end up with an exceptional success story.

MATTEL

The greatest drag racing duel of our time . . .

NEW! HOT WHEELS® MONGOOSE™ & SNAKE™ Drag Race Set #6438

Get in the driver's seat—for the super drag strip competition of the 70's as HOT WHEELS Cars presents the MONGOOSE & SNAKE Drag Race Set! A realistic recreation of this coast-to-coast racing struggle, MONGOOSE and SNAKE HOT WHEELS Cars lash out of the starting gate . . . swirl 360° thru the loop then burst past the straightaway and finish gate to pop drag 'chutes at the climax!

Only HOT WHEELS cars have the MONGOOSE and the SNAKE!

Get this:

1 HOT WHEELS MONGOOSE metal miniature car
1 HOT WHEELS SNAKE metal miniature car
2 Dare-Devil loops
2 Drag Chute Sets
1 Starting Gate
1 Finish Gate with Automatic Flag
32' Hot Strip Track
12 Joiners
1 Clamp
2 Matching Collector's Buttons
1 International Collector's Catalog

Std. Pack: 1/2 Doz. Wt: 8 Lbs.

Mattel sponsors the big ones! The MONGOOSE™ and SNAKE™, like miniature HOT WHEELS cars come to life—they're tearing up the track all over the nation.

Illustrated four-color package, 24" x 9" x 5"

HOT WHEELS presents the MONGOOSE and the SNAKE! Realistic racing machines right down to the decals! Mattel is the official sponsor of these two great cars.

HOT WHEELS Close-Up on The MONGOOSE

Tom "Mongoose" McEwen, 5-time holder of the national Speed and Elapsed Time drag records, is one of the most colorful performers in the sport.

A hot shoe since 16, Mongoose is a past titlist at Stardust Raceway National Open and Hot Rod Magazine Championship.

HOT WHEELS Spotlight of The SNAKE

Called "The Snake" because of his fast reactions at the starting line, Don Prudhomme is 1969's Driver of the Year.

Racing to more than a dozen drag championships last year, The Snake captured his second National Hot Rod Association title—and became one of only two drivers to win this coveted honor twice.

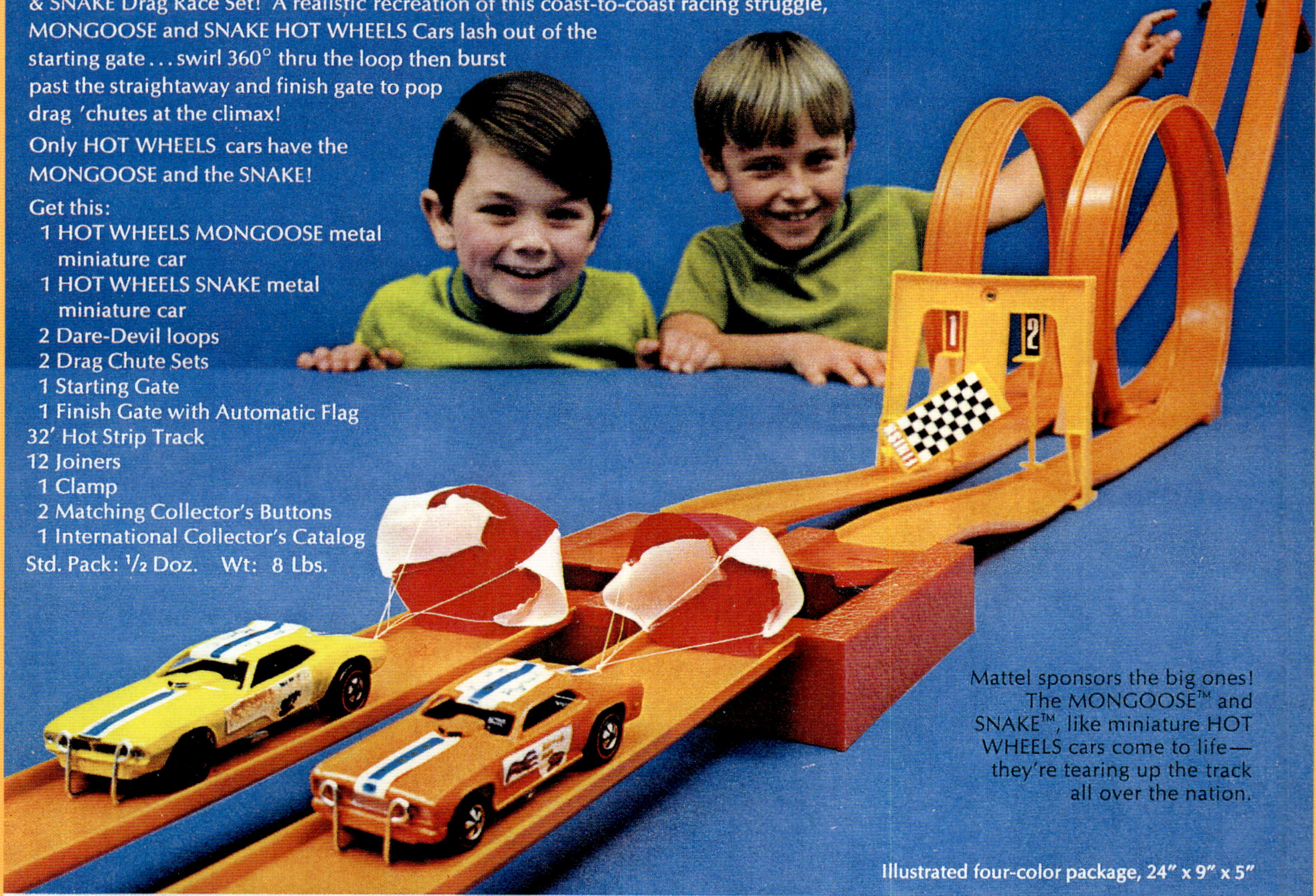

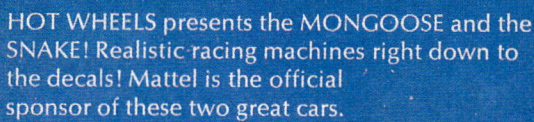

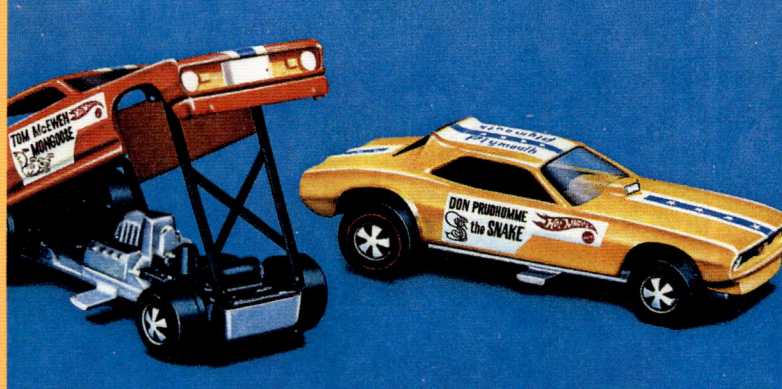

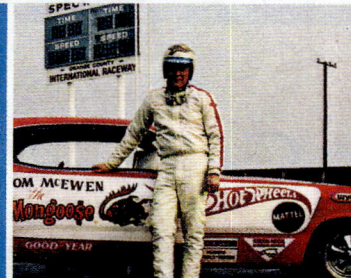

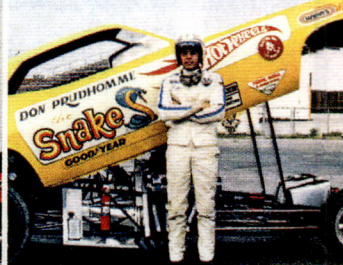

MONGOOSE® & SNAKE™
WILD WHEELIE SET #6037

MONGOOSE® & SNAKE®
Dragster Pak #5935

1 MONGOOSE I Dragster
1 SNAKE I Dragster
2 Balancer Tracks

Std. Pak: 24
Wt: 4 Lbs.

Authentically
styled rails!

Watch 'em
wheelie off the line!

BIG BELTER &
MATCHMAKER

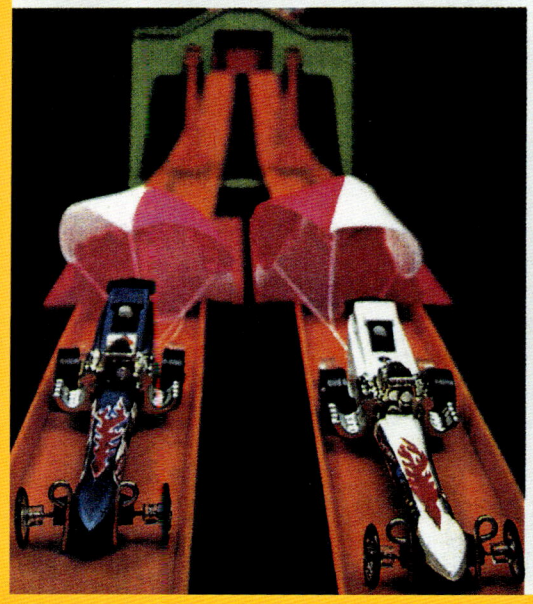

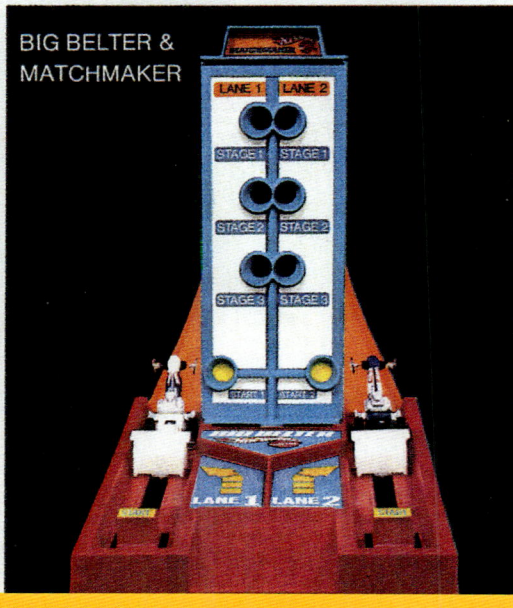

HOT STRIP
TRACK
SUPER
PAK
#6475

Std. Pak: 12
Wt: 14 Lbs.

Above, left, and opposite: Mattel Toy Company was the first non-automotive company to sponsor a race team, and the company's vision paid off when the Hot Wheels Snake vs. Mongoose program sold millions of the tiny cars. It was a time before video games and computers, when kids still played with toy cars. Mattel Toy Company advertised its toy cars as replicas of the real deal. According to designer Larry Wood, he actually measured and designed the cars as close to the actual cars as possible. The Snake and Mongoose funny cars featured a lift-up body shell, a chromed, supercharged engine, and full roll bars. The Hot Wheels sets included 360-degree Dare-Devil track loops so kids could race their cars like Snake and Mongoose. **Prudhomme Collection/Mattel, Inc.**

Above and opposite: Built by Exhibition Engineering, this is the real deal, one of only two Hot Wheels 'Cudas ever constructed. Its twin was destroyed in a top-end inferno. Prudhomme wasn't into the nostalgia craze at first, but as time went on, he understood the importance of the legacy he created. The Hot Wheels 'Cuda was certainly a milestone car. **Prudhomme Collection/Randy Fish**

Above and left: Recently, with the help of buddies Mike Kuhl and Steve Davis, Tom McEwen restored the original Hot Wheels Plymouth funny car to its 1970 condition. The car can be seen at shows and reunions. **Jim White/ McEwen Collection**

When the history of drag racing is reviewed many years from now, two warriors will be remembered as both fierce competitors and good friends. No doubt, the Snake vs. Mongoose rivalry changed drag racing forever.
Prudhomme Collection

CHAPTER 9

SNAKE VS. MONGOOSE UNPLUGGED

Author's note: The stars aligned, and Tom McEwen and Don Prudhomme agreed to meet with me and my tape recorder at the West Coast facility for Snake Racing in Vista, California. The idea was to get together and exchange comments about the Mattel Hot Wheels program in a face-to-face smackdown format and put to rest any misconceptions, spuriousness, falsification, or skullduggery conducted by either party. In reality, McEwen wanted to show up and make sure the Snake wasn't getting any more coverage in the book than he was.

The rules of engagement could not have been simpler. I would act as a monitor, asking questions about the Hot Wheels years in an alternate format, and their responses would be captured on tape.

Those rules lasted about one minute. My attempt to maintain order and calm turned into the equivalent of a 10-year-old trying to hold the attention of two 8-year-olds.

Finally things calmed and questioning began. Although much has been addressed in some form throughout other segments of the book, in this face-to-face exchange it seemed acceptable to allow some repetition of facts.

Author: Did the agreement with Mattel alter your racing agenda?

McEwen: We pretty much had our own schedule as I remember: the only thing that Mattel required us to do was to keep them posted as we moved from track to track so they could advise their public relations department and marketing people so they could set up displays. We usually had a good idea of where we were going, so when we arrived everything would be in place for us to show the cars, do some promotion, and maybe a radio or TV interview. Just to give some idea of how many places we would cover, I went through some of the old records and just couldn't believe what I read. From April 10 to the NHRA Nationals in September, we appeared at 28 different drag strips from Cecil County, Maryland, to Detroit, and from Milwaukee to Richmond, Virginia, and everywhere in between.

Prudhomme: I had gotten some idea of the booking thing on my tour with Tommy Ivo. I watched him deal with track promoters and learned the lessons on what to do and not do.

The Mattel Hot Wheels program did not place limits on McEwen or Prudhomme as to which races or tracks they could run. As a result (shown here) they ran both NHRA and AHRA events. At the AHRA events (one shown here at Scottsdale, Arizona) they would get appearance money. **Steve Reyes**

One big change brought on by the sponsorship program with Mattel Toy Company was that McEwen and Prudhomme had to learn to deal with the public, to present a professional appearance, and to consent to a never-ending barrage of TV and radio interviews. They took drag racing to a new level, on a par with NASCAR and Indianapolis. McEwen (right) loved talking and promoting his cause; Prudhomme tolerated the job. **Prudhomme Collection**

Also, Lynn and I went barnstorming around the country before the deal with Mattel. So, when we started with Mattel, we already had a schedule set up and knew many of the track promoters and what we could expect. The only real differences in the Hot Wheels program were the appearances at malls and shopping centers. And, the two of us did interviews together on the radio and TV to promote the Snake and Mongoose act.

Author: Did you enjoy or tolerate the Mattel promotion part of the program?

McEwen: Once we got started, it was actually great fun. Part of the program was for us to act as judges when the kids raced their Hot Wheels down those yellow tracks. We would make a big deal out of calling out the winners. Sometimes we would argue over the call, and the kids thought that was fun.

What Mattel did, that not many people know about, was that they held local events all over the country and ran eliminations according to age groups. Then there was some type of finals, and we would come in and show the cars, give out the trophies. The whole program was designed to sell toy cars. Man, we sold a lot of toy cars.

Author: What was it like touring together?

McEwen: We traveled together, stayed in the same motels, and went to the tracks together. When we came rolling in with those painted-up flatbed trucks and the cars mounted on them, it was a big deal. Even in the larger cities, people were impressed. It was before Speed Vision or cable TV and all the press coverage that racing gets today. Kids played with toys; they didn't have computer games and cell phones and laptops when they were 10 years old like today. We were some of the first teams to wear uniforms to the track. Some of the other racers would laugh, but we were hot, and it was just hard feelings because we got the big crowds. The kids would bring their Hot Wheels and be so pumped about getting up close to the cars and us.

Author: Did the bookings differ from track to track?

Prudhomme: Most of our match races were pretty simple. A track owner would book us for a two-out-of-three race, pay us when we appeared. At some tracks, under the IHRA or AHRA sanction we sometimes had to run with other cars that had been booked in for a show. Usually it was an eight-funny-car show, with the hope that the Snake and Mongoose would end up in the final. If it was a small field I usually won my side and hoped that Tom took care of his side.

McEwen: Yeah, Snake would win his races and I would help sweep the track and wipe his tires in the final ...

Author: Who did the kids really like best?

McEwen: Let me tell you, the Snake and Mongoose thing

was pretty evenly split. There were brothers who would fight each other about who was best. The wildest story ever was a couple of brothers up in Denver. We were racing outside Denver, and it was a big deal for the local track, so after the race Mattel wanted us to hang around, sign autographs, and so they set up a booth, and we are sitting there talking to the fans. These two guys, about 18 years old, muscular builds, no shirts, come walking up. One guy has a tattoo of the Snake and the other brother has the Mongoose. Each guy has a circle drawn on his arm, and they want us to sign right in the circle. They tell me as soon as we sign they are headed to the local tattoo parlor to get our names inked for good.

Prudhomme: I remember having a few girls come up and want their bodies signed. It was hard to say no, but I was married.

McEwen: Yeah.

Author: According to interviews, neither of you ever talked about arranging the outcome of a match race to save equipment or make things seem more equal. Is that true?

McEwen: People, especially the press guys, never believed that we didn't fix races. Well, I'm here to tell you straight up that we raced to win. No bullshit involved. The fans deserved to see us run our best, and we always did. I would have been better off if we would have [fixed races].

Prudhomme: I'm so glad, to this day, that we did it the way we ran. Because if we would have set something up where one of us won, it would have been like cheating. Fixing a race would have been a tough thing for me to handle. I hate losing so much that if I would have let Tom win a race, I couldn't have looked at myself in the mirror. It was a good thing, because when one of us won a race, we deserved the victory.

Author: Was the second year of the Mattel Hot Wheels program more successful than year one?

Prudhomme: Yeah, because we had new cars, real race cars. Little John Buttera built the second-generation Hot Wheels cars, and suddenly we could run harder and faster. It wasn't so important in the match race thing, but at national events, when we had to run [against] the other top funny cars, we could compete.

McEwen: The first cars were actually designed by the art department at Mattel. When they drew the concept, they put the wing on the roof. We didn't know any better, so we put it on the real car. I had flown the *Hemi 'Cuda* a few years earlier but never knew that it was because of the shape of the car.

Prudhomme: I remember saying, "That looks cool," not thinking that it might kill us. Neither the artist nor we knew anything about aerodynamics.

McEwen: The first cars had full round steering wheels, what does that tell you about having the hot setup? Nobody knew

Above and opposite: Not slaves to fashion, Tom and Don display some typical racetrack outerwear; the Snake checks out the track surface wearing fire suit pants and boots while the Mongoose directs a car after a burnout. Check the nifty sponsor pants. **Steve Reyes**

much about funny cars, and everything we did was a first-time experiment. I remember when you jumped on the gas our first cars would go everywhere but straight. It took us time to figure out what to do to get those cars to run strong, and, by the time we did, all the new technology was in the newest cars that we were running against.

Author: What was the true story about the dragsters? Did you like them or not?

McEwen: That was an idea from Mattel. But the truth of the matter is that Snake never really wanted to go Funny Car racing. If it had been up to him we would have run dragsters from the start. It was the money that changed his mind. Mattel didn't really ask us our opinion. The design department came up with a second-generation Hot Wheels game called *Wild Wheelie* sets. It was a pair of dragsters with wheelie bars that did a wheel stand at the start and when they crossed the finish line little

parachutes came out. Mattel wanted us to have both funny cars and the dragsters.

Prudhomme: I think that Mattel got the idea from the fact that I ran my Fuel dragster whenever I could. Sometimes I would tow the dragster trailer behind the Hot Wheels truck. Dragsters were still very popular, although the funny cars were taking over, but I liked the idea of running a dragster, especially when Mattel was going to be paying for it.

McEwen: I was doing the same thing, so all we did was refit my Woody Gilmore car and his Don Long car with those slab bodies. Tom Hanna did the aluminum for the bodies, but it didn t make them any less ugly. I think we got paid to make the switch and for the paint and body panels. After that they were just part of the program.

Author: This segment of the questioning is directed at the Mongoose. After 1973, Mattel became an associate sponsor and

The Snake vs. Mongoose rivalry was considered the biggest thing to hit drag racing since the sport began. The pair match raced at tracks all over the United States in addition to hitting the big-time national events like the NHRA Gatornationals. **Prudhomme Collection**

In year two of the Hot Wheels program, the Mattel Toy Company introduced a new game called **Mongoose & Snake Wild Wheelie Set**. In turn, both Snake and Mongoose built full-size versions to promote the program. Lucky for the boys, the dragsters used chassis from cars that were hanging out in their race shops. **Steve Reyes**

more or less allowed the Hot Wheels promotion to move in other directions. And, according to interviews, a new deal was constructed with Beechnut Gum to carry the Care Free gum logo on the cars, making each character a different flavor. According to the Snake, he got all the gum and the Mongoose got the money. True or not true?

McEwen: Look around, does it look like he didn't get any money? He has a shop in California and one in Indianapolis. I have only one house. No airplane. Trust me, the Snake always gets paid.

[Author's note: Halfway through the discussion, with things going along at a fairly civilized tone, it was time to turn up the heat and begin to uncover some of the personal anecdotes that have missed the pages of the magazines. It didn't take much to get the boys to show a little Snake vs. Mongoose behind-the-scenes magic.]

Author: Is there anything about the Mattel Hot Wheels years that either of you would like to talk about?

McEwen: Looking back, it was like a marriage in many ways. We had our good times and bad times. Because of the competition being what it was and the fact that we had to answer to Mattel for the programs we presented, there were times when both of us had to swallow our pride, shut down our egos, and just do the job. I'll admit that he won more races than I did. He was more mechanical that I was and spent far more time working on the car. I enjoyed the people part. As for getting the car ready, I depended on the crew. I hated getting my hands all greasy and my knuckles beat up.

Prudhomme: He hated getting dirty. I would tell him nobody likes getting dirty, but it's part of the job.

McEwen: What the public doesn't understand is the Snake was a happily married man, so I had to go out and take care of business, support my reputation as a ladies' man. That's hard work and takes dedication.

Although Pruchomme has stated that he didn't like the slab-side fuel dragsters designed by Mattel for the **Wild Wheelie** game, he did win some races during the short time the car competed. **Steve Reyes**

If you were to ask who won the most races, Snake or Mongoose, the answer would be Snake, if you ask Prudhomme. However, McEwen counters by saying that the Snake won more, but the Mongoose won the most important races. It is a never-ending source of entertainment.
Steve Reyes

Prudhomme: This is the God's honest truth. He had this briefcase that he carried. You would think that it was full of government secrets the way he guarded it. He had a way of opening it, like Agent 007 exposing his case loaded with all those cool weapons. His case was filled with gold chains; he would pass them out to the girls he met. The chains were good for about 36 hours before they would turn your neck green. He broke a lot of hearts back then. It was good that we kept moving.

One time I'm working on an engine block in the parking lot of this motel we were staying at back in the Midwest. It was the dead of summer, and by 8:00 in the morning it's 80 degrees with 100 percent humidity. I'm honing a block with an electric motor and a honing stone; I had been up most of the night, I'm tired and sweating and cussing. Finally, I throw down the drill, walk over to the rooms, bang on the Mongoose's door and start yelling, "Get your lazy ass out here and get to work." I hear a woman's voice from inside say,

"Tommy will be out in a minute." That was touring with McEwen.

I was so mad that I tell McEwen, "You wait until tonight; I'm going to kick your butt in front of a crowd. No wonder you never win any races!" I was hot.

McEwen: You must have me mixed up with somebody else. I spent my time promoting and trying to make money for our program.

Author: Speaking of bad times, what was the worst moment during the Mattel tour?

McEwen: Snake's fire in Seattle, but he should tell you because I was in the pit area loading up to go home early.

Prudhomme: We were at Seattle Raceway, and I can't remember if it was a 64-car show, but it was a big Funny Car race. I was in the final round against the *L.A. Hooker*, not a girl but the funny car. At the time, we were running our John Buttera–built Hot Wheels cars. We take off, and my car hooks up and I'm on a run.

Above: Mattel Toy Company celebrated the 35th Anniversary of the Hot Wheels Snake vs. Mongoose program at the NHRA facility in Pomona, California, with a dinner and showing of the original funny cars, now totally restored. As you can see, time has treated the Mongoose (left) and the Snake (right) well. **McEwen Collection/Randy Fish**

145

Right and below: During the Hot Wheels program, the boys raced up to four times a week, on every type of track, all over the country without many unpleasant experiences. However, at Seattle during an NHRA meet, Prudhomme had one of the all-time biggest engine explosions and a huge fire. Not only was the fire world-class, but the car flew, setting a personal altitude record. **Prudhomme Collection/Neely's Photo Service**

There are a couple of things I should make note of before I finish the story. Back then we were still running a coil-over shock on the front suspension, so, at speed, under a load, the front end had a tendency to rise up slightly, or at least it would flex. Also, on the run previous I had scorched a piston. We had conducted a pressure check on the cylinders, and one cylinder was down on compression, indicating that it was losing pressure. But, the crew figured that it would be good for one more round.

Just as I got to the lights there was a huge bang, and the engine let go and I was engulfed in flames. The idea of a fire in a funny back in those days was commonplace, so for the first instant it wasn't the fire that bothered me. I figured it would come down when I hit the fire bottles (onboard fire suppression system). What got my attention was a feeling that I was in the air. The car was flying. The front end had come up, and suddenly everything got quiet and I couldn't believe what was happening. The next thing I knew I was 15 feet in the air. The concussion from the engine explosion had knocked me halfway unconscious, and when the car hit the ground I went totally out from the impact. My back was jammed into the seat so hard I thought it was broken. Luckily the body blew off and took most of the fire with it as it disintegrated. Man, that was a big hit.

Because we didn't know much about aerodynamics, it took a while to find out that the fire ate up all of the oxygen under the car—that air pressure keeps the car stable so when the downforce went away it was game over.

At the end of the track the car came rolling to a stop, and I had no idea what had gone on. We rebuilt the car, and recently I restored the car and it will find its way into a museum. Kenny Youngblood [world-famous automotive artist] created a full-on painting of that crash. It was bad business.

Author: What about some final thoughts?

Prudhomme: I don't know about Tom and his feelings, but I can honestly say our Hot Wheels time was the best time in drag racing. Not just for us, but for everyone involved. Because the late '60s and early '70s was the time when drag racing took off and became a big-time sport.

McEwen: Overall, we had a great time. Sure, there were occasions when we had our differences, but I wouldn't trade a day.

When you think about it, the people we met, the travel, the places we got to see, it was a great experience. At the time, we would have never seen the country the way we did if it hadn't been for the Hot Wheels program.

Prudhomme: I'll tell you, we spent three years involved with Mattel and the Hot Wheels deal, and to this day it's remained the biggest thing the two of us have ever done.

McEwen: People still talk about Hot Wheels and Snake vs. Mongoose. When you ask around the sport, all of the journalists who work on the magazines and even the management at NHRA admit that the Snake vs. Mongoose rivalry was the single biggest thing to hit the sport.

It wasn't just in drag racing that we were popular. The kids liked the characters. and there was carryover into TV commercials and cartoon shows.

Prudhomme: Today, fans say, "Hey, why don't they have the rivalry in drag racing like the old days?" John Force is about the biggest thing going. He is kind of a throwback to the early days, but he doesn't have anybody hating him. Back in the day, everybody had a nickname, and the fans rooted for their favorites and booed the ones they hated. It was cool.

McEwen: The Snake and Mongoose thing goes back to the early days of our drag racing careers. I remember I would go over to the body shop where he worked in my Oldsmobile Fiesta station wagon; all lowered with custom wheels, tinted windows, and pinstriping on the fenders and doors. I would have the air conditioning on and would see him working all covered with paint and primer dust. He'd be sanding a car, sweat running down in his eyes, the 100-degree San Fernando Valley sun beating on his head, and I would crack the window about an inch and say, "Hey, you got time for lunch?" He would look up, and his eyes would burn a hole in a steel plate, and he would answer, "Get the hell out of here, I'm working. I'm not like you."

It all went downhill from there.

Now I call him every week or so just to tell him how bitchin' he is. It helps his ego.

> **"Overall, we had a great time. Sure there were occasions when we had our differences, but I wouldn't trade a day."**

The rivalry that changed drag racing did not begin with the thought of making history; it was just two young racers trying to make a living doing what they loved. **Prudhomme Collection**

EPILOGUE

Every story, no matter how long or abbreviated, must inevitably reach its conclusion. The story of the Snake and the Mongoose is no exception.

During the peak of the Hot Wheels program, as editor of a monthly car magazine, I didn't have much time to dwell on the impact Tom McEwen and Don Prudhomme were having on the children of America. To us in the media, they were just two more funny car drivers.

Going back one step further, I had met both Tom McEwen and Don Prudhomme at the various Southern California drag strips during events we raced together. I would see Prudhomme at Tony Nancy's shop or Kent Fuller's chassis business. McEwen hung out at Keith Black Racing Engines, or sometimes he could be found at Mickey Thompson's speed shop and manufacturing facility in Long Beach. We were all part of the scene— drag racers trying to make names for ourselves.

Back then, all the drivers were concerned with image; we were all young, ego-driven, and more than a bit cocky. Driving a fuel-burning dragster was not for everyone, and all the drivers enjoyed pushing the other guy just to see his reaction. After all, it was the 1960s, life was lived a little further over on the wild side, and a little intimidation Thursday afternoon could go a long way if you found yourself lined up across from that driver Saturday night.

Still, like members of a huge family, drag racers looked after their own. Grab a copy of a 1960s-era *Hot Rod* magazine or one of the drag racing newspapers of the day and check out the Top Fuel teams—they were friends, not paid crewmembers. Everyone got his or her name on the car; sponsors could be anyone offering help with parts, maybe a local speed shop, a service station, or an inventor trying to sell an idea.

There was room both for those who would someday become legends and for those who labored in obscurity. There were no barriers between the classes. No elite status for anyone unless you earned respect. You could actually walk into shops owned by Keith Black, Ed Pink, Louie Senter, Ed Iskenderian, Ed Donovan, Kent Fuller, Woody Gilmore, Tony Nancy, Frank Huszar, Kent Enderle, Art Chrisman, Stu Hilborn, Bob Sorrell, and countless other now-famous names and talk one-on-one about what you needed and how much you could afford. Only two things mattered to all the teams who raced: how fast did you run, and how brave was your driver.

Both McEwen and Prudhomme drove many different drag racing machines in their careers, but they will always be remembered for the Hot Wheels funny cars that served as models for the Snake vs. Mongoose toys. Here you can see the McEwen funny car (top) and Prudhomme in the Greer, Black, and Prudhomme Top Fuel dragster (lower). **Steve Reyes**

150

On the opposite side of the pit area from those who would become famous were the no-names, the dedicated racers giving their all simply for the pure pleasure of the sport. There were so many of them, the weekend warriors who came and went, each leaving a tiny piece of his soul scattered among the empty oil cans, broken parts, and unfulfilled dreams found at the strip on Monday morning.

The decade of the 1960s was epic: sex, drugs, rock 'n' roll, anti-war and civil rights movements, peace and love, hippies, the assassination of a president, and humans landing on the moon all coexisted with, and might have had effects on, drag racing. Drag racing became more serious, faster, and quicker; somehow it increased in sensuality, while at the same time it became more cruel and unforgiving. Gone were the innocent, carefree days of the 1950s, replaced by a new image: hip, cocky, more daring, less fearful of consequence. This change in character was most noticeable in the Top Fuel dragster class. Drivers of fuel-burning dragsters moved themselves into an elite position—they were the stars of the show. Don Prudhomme and Tom McEwen were part of that world of change, and its effects would test their mettle and help determine the direction of their future efforts.

Alongside the harshness that came with the 1960s, the beast called the Fuel dragster took on a beautiful new form. Artful grace in the form of full-flowing bodies covered the deadly consequence of pushing a nitromethane-charged bomb too far. The cars became long and stunningly beautiful, the show became more spectacular, and suddenly the magic missiles were going well over 200 miles per hour in a quarter-mile. For some, the lure and seduction of hero worship overwhelmed good judgment, and egos rose to soaring heights.

For others, pushing the limits brought a harvest of pain and suffering. It was a time to beware. An old mechanic friend of mine named Dave Sowins, who would go to the races with me to make sure I didn't get into trouble, used to say, "Don't let the

bullshit turn your blue eyes brown. The object of this exercise is to get down the track before the other guy; nothing matters except reaching that goal. You can't talk your way into winning, there is no time out, no second lap, just one shot, win or go home. And I don't want to go home yet." With that bit of advice in mind, on any given Saturday night, the collective world of Southern California drag racers would show up at their favorite strips of asphalt to do battle.

Back in the day, there was a highly prized ritual to running a front-engine, fuel-burning dragster. The ritual began with a push start, an act of proof that you were committed to what was about to take place. For the fans it was just a very cool thing to witness. Nearly every track allowed the Fuel dragsters to be pushed down to the far end of the drag strip. The time required to come back from the end of the track to the starting line allowed the track announcers to tell the crowd the highlights of your car and build up a little tension.

It always felt a little confined as you sat waiting. The bulky aluminized fire suit, oversized protective boots, restrictive facemask, helmet, glass-lens goggles, and safety harness created an adaptation of claustrophobia. It was difficult to keep your eyes from staring at the back of the blower, which was sitting only two feet in front of your face. Most cars had the driver's legs placed over the rear-end housing, with the throttle and clutch pedals straddling a clutch can that might or might not contain the effects of an exploding flywheel and clutch assembly. Because air intake was restricted by your facemask and goggles, it was easy to doze off slightly as you waited for the track announcer to call out the words, "And now going down the strip to fire up, running out of so-and-so speed shop … "

Then there was a tiny sensation that ignited your every fiber: the touch of the push truck against the push bar of your car. As the motion began, familiar noises set the ritual into a rhythm; first the rear-end gears howl, then once the clutch is engaged, the engine begins to emit all sorts of clicks and whirling. Starting a Fuel

> **As the motion began, familiar noises set the ritual into a rhythm; first the rear-end gears howl, then, once the clutch is engaged, the engine begins to emit all sorts of clicks and whirling.**

Above and right: McEwen once remarked that the sponsorship of Mattel Toy Company allowed him and Prudhomme to build cars with the best equipment and hire the best crews. In all of the match races and NHRA National events the Snake and Mongoose ran, only once was there a serious accident. *Ed Justice Jr./Author Collection*

Prudhomme's U.S. Smokeless Tobacco Company dragster finished second in the NHRA POWERade standings in 2008. **Randy Fish**

Before Prudhomme became involved with the Hot Wheels program, he drove the wild-running SOHC Ford owned by Lou Baney. Sponsored by Carroll Shelby and with an engine built by Ed Pink, the car had once been driven by McEwen. The car began life with a Hemi, then got a Ford Cammer engine when they were first introduced. McEwen broke in the new Cammer, but it never really ran properly for him. As a consequence, in trying to get every advantage he could despite the not-yet-sorted engine, McEwen had a series of disqualifications due to leaving the line on the red light. This incensed Baney, who eventually replaced the Mongoose with the Snake—and turned up the heat between the two. **Steve Reyes**

Above and below: Tom McEwen traded the Mattel Hot Wheels Plymouth for a Coors Beer–sponsored Corvette at the conclusion of the Mattel Toy Company contract. **Steve Reyes**

Above and opposite: Two of the more unusual cars driven by the Snake and the Mongoose are shown here. Prudhomme is driving the rear-engine **Yellow Feather** fuel dragster, and McEwen is in the Kent Fuller–built and Gene Adams–powered **Shark Car. Steve Reyes**

dragster in those days was a matter of engaging the clutch, adding a touch or bath of fuel, making sure the oil pressure was up, and flipping the magneto switch. The engine would bark to life and immediately begin to expel raw nitro out of the headers into the face of the driver. In those days two cars would come down to the starting line together, make a U-turn, and roll to the starting line ready to stage. It was at this point a driver might realize that the beautiful car that moments earlier had displayed only quiet elegance was now a wild beast unleashed, capable of hurting, burning, maiming, or killing its driver unless controlled with great skill.

As Tom McEwen put it, "I'd like to see some of today's drivers do what we had to do. You would leave the starting line, and the car would go everywhere but straight. The headers would be blowing back in your face, your goggles would get coated with oil, tire smoke made it impossible to see, and there was a bomb in front of your face ready to go off as you approached 220 miles per hour. You had to work the clutch [no computer] to keep the tires from going up in smoke and try and stay in control until you got through the lights. Then grab the chute release and hope for the best. It took commitment to drive a Top Fuel car in the '60s."

There are more feelings to remember, but as the saying goes, "You just had to be there."

For sure, Mattel's Hot Wheels program that featured the Snake and the Mongoose put drag racing on the map and opened the door for a flood of non-automotive-industry sponsors to enter the picture. Corporate America came to drag racing on the heels of an idea dreamed up by Tom McEwen. And, drag racing is better for the effort.

As for the boys, McEwen is still involved in drag racing as the director of motorsports at *Drag Racer* magazine. He also races his own fantastic line of quarter horse champions; all of his horses carry the name "Mongoose" somewhere in their titles.

The Snake remains in professional NHRA Top Fuel racing as an owner. For the 2009 and 2010 seasons he will field a Top Fuel dragster driven by former IHRA champion Spencer Massey, sponsored by U.S. Smokeless and a host of associate sponsors. Prudhomme can be found on the starting line, toothpick firmly installed, at all of the NHRA National events. He is still the Snake.

For me, the 50 years I've known the Snake and the Mongoose have gone by much too quickly, but those years have brought me a better understanding of what life is all about. Life is about giving of yourself and always playing fair. Tom McEwen and Don Prudhomme have done both.

INDEX